Care
Literacy
Equity / social justice
Ethical leadership
Community
Excellence
diversity

"Learning Community"
Continuous improvement
Safety

Leadership Standards in Action

Leadership Standards in Action

The School Principal as Servant-Leader

Cade Brumley

Rowman & Littlefield Education
A division of
ROWMAN & LITTLEFIELD PUBLISHERS, INC.
Lanham • Boulder • New York • Toronto • Plymouth, UK

Published by Rowman & Littlefield Education
A division of Rowman & Littlefield Publishers, Inc.
A wholly owned subsidiary of
The Rowman & Littlefield Publishing Group, Inc.
4501 Forbes Boulevard, Suite 200, Lanham, Maryland 20706
http://www.rowmaneducation.com

Estover Road, Plymouth PL6 7PY, United Kingdom

British Library Cataloguing in Publication Information Available

Library of Congress Cataloging-in-Publication Data

Brumley, Cade, 1981-
Leadership standards for action : the school principal as servant-leader / Cade Brumley. p. cm.
Summary: "case studies of exceptional principals as servant-leaders"-- Provided by publisher.
Includes bibliographical references and index.
ISBN 978-1-61048-390-2 (hardback) -- ISBN 978-1-61048-391-9 (paper) -- ISBN 978610483926 (ebook)
1. School principals--United States--Case studies. 2. Educational leadership--United States--Case studies. 3. Servant leadership--Case studies. I. Title.
LB2831.92.B82 2011
371.2'012--dc23
2011041894

Printed in the United States of America

This book is dedicated to the past, present, and future principals as servant-leaders of the DeSoto and Sabine Parish School Systems. Your work in the daily trenches of reality has been, is, or will be a priceless combination of science and art.

Contents

Acknowledgments

Respectfully, I appreciate the invaluable feedback and support given this project by Beth, Bridgette, Gary, Mona, Patrick, and Shirley.

Humbly, I remain a daily servant-leader for Toni, Preston, and Braden.

Foreword

What do we represent as leaders? Who do we represent as leaders? Are we responsible? For what and to whom? If there is a leader responsibility, it at least begins with the moment when a need to hear these questions, to take them upon oneself as leader and respond, is imposed. This imperative for responding is the initial form and minimal requirement of responsibility one takes on as servant-leader and as a principal in schools today. In *Leadership Standards in Action: The School Principal as Servant-Leader*, Cade Brumley reminds the reader of the responsibilities of leadership in an era of increasing complexity in education.

The rapidly changing social and economic conditions in society today call for a new kind of leadership, which should be capable of maximizing opportunities and optimizing resources, and at the same time a kind of leadership that serves the public needs and the needs of students who enter the school each day to learn and grow. Simply stated, the principal in today's school operates within a system of ever-increasing complexities, influenced by the breakdown of the nuclear family, frequent paradigm shifts within society, and an increased responsibility to perform in an era of educational accountability, particularly wherein standards have become a hallmark of our educational system and the practice of educators.

In his work, *Leadership Standards in Action: The School Principal as Servant-Leader*, Brumley draws this last point into specific relief as he focuses on the value of standards for educational administration in shaping leadership praxis, carefully examining the meaning of standards-based leadership through a carefully crafted and accessible theoretical lens of servant-leadership.

Brumley builds a logical and pragmatic argument for the ISLLC standards, acknowledging that the standards have gained in importance over the last decade. Each chapter seeks to illuminate an operational framework guided by one of six ISLLC standards, and provide clarity of responsibility for the principal as servant-leader. In authoring each chapter, Brumley has cogently argued that principal practices should find alignment, either directly or indirectly, within the ISLLC standards. Principals who satisfy each of the standards should be considered highly effective principals within their field.

That said, the clarifying, and perhaps major importance, found within *Leadership Standards in Action: The School Principal as Servant-Leader* is the

articulation of servant-leadership represented by Brumley's deep examination through the theoretical lens of servant-leadership, of each standard as a framework for understanding principal practices. It is in the
weaving of servant-leadership theory into this examination, while draw-
ing from real-life principal leader experiences, that Brumley directs the
reader to understanding the role of the principal as servant-leader.

In reading each chapter, I am reminded of the deep-seated nature of
being a servant—authenticity and at the same time a form of spirituality—which Herman Hesse's (1956) novel, *The Journey to the East* elicits for
the reader. For Herman Hesse and Cade Brumley alike, whether a Sherpa
guide on the side of mountain or the principal in the school, a servant-
leader is one who consciously chooses to lead through service to others.
The servant-leader finds a belief in and connection to something greater
than oneself. It is this connection to leaders' heart and intuition that reveals his or her capacity for leadership.

Brumley, in examining standards-based servant-leadership, applies
both a philosophy and standards-based model of principal practice to
help the readers understand that principals must follow a path that is
reasoned and logical and at the same time a path that is illuminated by an
understanding that the servant-leader is servant first. Standards provide
a reasoned path, whereas being a servant begins with the natural feeling
that one wants to serve.

The challenge of servant-leadership is to rise above the day-to-day
administrative and managerial concerns and focus on the larger purpose
of the work and the school organization. Brumley directs the reader, in
each chapter, to an understanding of the larger purpose of the principal's
work in the school.

Written carefully in the text and chapters of *Leadership Standards in
Action: The School Principal as Servant-Leader* is a deep-seated reflection of
what Robert Greenleaf, in his 1977 seminal text, *Servant-Leadership: A
Journey into the Nature of Legitimate Power and Greatness*, posited as the
philosophical underpinnings of servant-leadership. Greenleaf was
among the first to analyze the qualities of leaders and followers, and the
necessity for leaders to be attentive to the needs of others.

Servant-leaders, as Greenleaf explained, constantly inquire whether
other people's highest priority needs are being served. Do those served
grow as people? Do they, while being served, become healthier, wiser,
freer, more autonomous, more likely themselves to become servants?
Brumley has carefully woven the thoughts of Greenleaf into the chapters
of his book. Importantly, he has directed the reader to consider the questions, offered by Greenleaf, as an implicit guide for principals who seek
to embrace standards-based servant-leadership.

What Brumley does well in the each of the chapters is reflect to the
reader that servant-leadership is an inner quality as much as an exercise

of "legitimate" authority. It is as much a path of service as it is a path guided by standards of practice.

Over the past decade, the ISLLC Standards for Educational Administration have become increasingly recognized as a universal structure to guide the thoughts and actions of school principals seeking to increase school performance and improve individual student achievement. More recently, caring and passionate principals throughout the United States have become intrigued by, or interested in, the idea of leadership as a vehicle for whole-school improvement and, from a humanistic standpoint, a moral obligation to fulfill. Brumley situates effective leadership within the framework of the six ISLLC standards for educational administration, illuminating how principals might successfully lead as serving the needs of the school while adhering, with fidelity, to the standards.

Principals, as leaders, are expected to be ethical in their responsibilities and at the same time see their work as a gift of oneself to a common cause, a higher calling in the service of the public. Conveyed to the reader within each chapter of *Leadership Standards in Action: The School Principal as Servant-Leader* is a sense that true servant-leaders are required to be selfless and the same time they are required to follow a reasoned path.

Due to the growing popularity of servant-leadership over the past decade, and the increasing prominence of ISLLC standards, it was imperative to take steps to not only explore the meaning of student-leadership but to examine the effectiveness of a leadership model that connects both standards and philosophy. Although there are an increasing number of books on leadership published each year, few hold the promise of Brumley's *Leadership Standards in Action: The School Principal as Servant-Leader* for appropriately preparing principals. What distinguishes Brumley's work is that he moves beyond the theoretical and presents a more authentic and servant-oriented approach to leadership development and practice that blends the importance of standards and the spirit of service.

We live in a world made increasingly complex and problematic by conflicting political and ideological agendas, changing demographics, and economic tensions. And in this world, education is the common ground for all children and parents regardless of race, ethnicity, gender, sexual orientation, language, or socioeconomic status. At the school level, holding this common ground is the work of the principal as servant-leader, work that is at once challenging and vital to the well-being of all. Preparing principals for the work of standards-based servant-leadership requires insight and understanding of standards and equally of the complex responsibilities associated with a principal's work.

The need for a book that brings to the foreground a level of pragmatic insight grounded in experience and tempered by understanding is without question, and *Leadership Standards in Action: The School Principal as Servant-Leader* meets this need, providing the reader with a window into the reality of the principal's work. Brumley demystifies the nature of being a "servant" while examining the "reality" of the principalship, bringing clarity of vision and understanding through his examination of the different dimensions of the principal's work defined through educational leadership standards.

Standards elicit a sense of ethical "self" in the shaping of leadership practice. Embracing a *servant* sense of self complements the ethical "self," forming a stronger sense or responsibility as principal and servant-leader. These are points made explicit throughout each chapter.

What becomes apparent in reading about standards-based servant-leadership is the necessity to continuously ask oneself: What do I represent as a principal, as a school leader? Whom do I represent as principal, as a school leader? Am I responsible? For what and to whom? These appear to be more implicit in the chapters, yet stand as explicit responsibilities of the servant-leader following a standards-based path of practice.

In closing, it is important to note that Brumley's *Leadership Standards in Action: The School Principal as Servant-Leader* offers both professors, students of principal-preparation programs, and practicing school principals a well-written and critically insightful work on the complex world of work associated with principal leadership. Each chapter directs the reader to real-life experiences of the building administrator, providing an authentic and honest look at what it means to be a servant-leader and principal in today's schools.

Tempered by an understanding of and value for theory made relevant in a practical and accessible manner, and practice demonstrated with experience-based scenarios, the reader will find lessons of the servant-leader that illuminate what it means to follow the path of ISLLC standards as a servant-leader. And, as in Herman Hesse's *The Journey to the East*, the principal as servant-leader will find wisdom and practical meaning that may be applied to his or her own journey into leadership.

Dr. Patrick M. Jenlink
Professor of Doctoral Studies
Department of Secondary Education and Educational Leadership
Stephen F. Austin State University
June 7, 2011

Part 1

Leadership

ONE
Principal Leadership

If I can stop one heart from breaking, I shall not live in vain. If I can ease one life the aching, Or cool one pain, Or help one fainting robin Unto his nest again, I shall not live in vain. — Emily Dickinson

THE PRINCIPALSHIP = A CALLING

When he was an elementary school student, his mother worked in the school cafeteria as a food-service employee. Each morning, well before the break of dawn, they loaded the car and headed toward school. Along the way, they stopped and picked up an elderly lady from the community who volunteered her time in the school cafeteria. She did not have transportation, so his mother gave her a lift. Once they arrived at school, the ladies began their work of preparing a *real* breakfast for the students.

He stayed in the cafeteria with his mom until the principal stirred in the main building. Once he saw the first lights illuminate the classrooms and hallways, he jaunted off to the principal's aid. During his elementary-school years, he recalls having three different principals, and all were willing, to one extent or another, to indulge his tagging along with them. Sometimes they let him make teacher-lounge coffee, sometimes he got to raise the American flag on the flagpole, and he was always welcomed to the morning newspaper. He was on campus and active well before any other student—he felt privileged for the opportunity.

When children are asked, *What do you want to be when you grow up?* they typically provide a plethora of interesting responses. The first time he considered his answer was during first grade as the teacher went one by one through the rows, asking students to express interest in future vocations. Some of his friends were commenting about being professional basketball players, movie stars, or rocket scientists.

He remembers thinking, *I'm going to be a school principal.* He truly had no idea what a school principal was aside from his morning time on campus, or what a school principal actually did once the school day began. He thought it was pretty cool, though, how the principal got to use the intercom to speak to everyone and dismiss the buses with the wave of an arm.

He is not certain why he was drawn to this work at such a young age other than a belief that he was called to serve and this illuminated an obvious pathway. Along the way, he decided the principalship was the job for him and never looked back. He earned multiple degrees, culminating with a doctoral degree in educational leadership. He believes that leaders entering the principalship with a pure heart are answering a call to provide, a call to fulfill, a call to serve.

During his service as a professional educator, he has had the good fortune to serve in multiple capacities. He started his career as a substitute teacher during his college days and became a full-time teacher/coach upon graduation. After a few years, he became an assistant principal and two years later, he assumed the principalship of a PK–12 combination school (the same school he attended as a student).

Serving as the principal of that school was the most difficult and yet most rewarding job of his educational career: that school had captured his heart. After some great successes, thanks to the team that surrounded him, he accepted a position at the district level. His path was, and remains, one of humble beginnings, a glowing passion to find better ways, and a desire to serve others.

In case the mystery has not been solved, I was that boy and I am the man lucky enough to fulfill those dreams. The career sequence and experiences are not shared as a form of personal edification; instead, the information is provided as a basis of credibility for the following statement: *The school principalship is the most demanding, difficult, and oft-unwinnable position in the entire school system.* Simultaneously, despite the unending challenges of the job, the school principalship is a *rush of adrenaline* with a direct line of immediate influence upon numerous stakeholders, providing an enormous opportunity to fulfill the calling of service to others and vastly improve their lives.

In reflecting on working for principals, serving as a principal, on-site consulting with principals, and making presentations to principals, a single quote seems to accurately describe the scope of the school principalship. Fullan (2001) found that school principals must be "all things to all people" (p. 140). That quote could be expanded to include *all the time.* Individuals, either naïve or courageous, who enter the principalship can expect no less than a constant barrage of questions, problems, and issues that will frequently seem insurmountable. As experience deepens practitioner understanding, the ability to be proactive improves the daily work.

Effective principals view questioning as curiosity in action, problems as opportunities for improvement, and issues as possibilities for bringing people together toward commonality. Seasoned principals further realize that conflict is not necessarily a *bad* thing; instead, it acts as a catalyst for necessary change and can be ushered in accidentally or purposefully. The journey of the principalship is awesome in both responsibility and possibility for those committed individuals willing to replace *selfishness* with *selflessness* to improve the specific situations of individuals and the general plight of society as a whole.

FRAMING THE PRINCIPALSHIP

Boxing the school principal into a formal and universally accepted definition is futile work. There will seemingly always be discussion on who principals are, how they should be prepared, what requirements should be met for certification, what roles they should assume on campus, and what levels of power and authority they actually have available. In fact, even after having extensively researched the principalship and lived the principalship, we are still not sure what it is. We understand the principalship as a *position* but still struggle with conceptualizing the principalship as a *job*. Teschke (1996) believes "Except for principals themselves, very few people understand what it is that principals really do" (p. 2).

Even with spending years in training to become a school principal, most are totally unaware of the intensity of the daily work with both internal and external factors seeking to influence schooling processes for both negative and positive reasons. Most learn, however, that all school stakeholders have an *agenda*. Even those people who say *I don't have an agenda* actually do.

Some agendas are noble and some are driven by greed. It becomes the school principal's responsibility to carve every stakeholder's personal agenda into a collective vision for students. Fullan (2001) believes "There is no question that the demands on the principalship have become even more intensified over the past 10 years, 5 years, 1 year" (p. 141).

The work of the school principal is unbelievably difficult, but it provides the context for exceptionally rewarding achievements. Explaining the dynamic and diversified demands on school principals, Copland (2001) wrote the following fictional job description:

> Position Opening: School Principal, Anytown School District. Qualifications: wisdom of a sage, vision of a CEO, intellect of a scholar, leadership of a point guard, compassion of a counselor, moral strength of a nun, courage of a firefighter, craft knowledge of a surgeon, political savvy of a senator, toughness of a soldier, listening skills of a blind man, humility of a saint, collaborative skills of an entrepreneur, certitude of a civil rights activist, charisma of a stage performer, and the

Job Desc. of Prin.

patience of Job. (One might also add mathematical skills of an actuary). Salary lower than you might expect. (p. 528)

While Copland's advertisement is written in parody, much of the content is true. School principals are frequently expected to perform unreasonable tasks, especially when supplemental support resources are limited due to district budgetary constraints.

Examples of such *above and beyond* practices include removing pencil lead from skin, constantly fixing broken eyeglasses, exterminating vermin, driving bus routes, organizing dusty book rooms, clearing clogged toilets, and teaching classes during a teacher's maternity leave. As foul and uncomfortable as some of those experiences are, they help mold the principalship into one of service to others. Nothing says authenticity like grabbing disinfectant cleaner, a pair of latex gloves, and a broom and leading the charge to eradicate the school of whatever grossness might be displayed in the school hallway.

True Desc.

School leadership, as stated by Keith and Girling (1991) is a "highly complex phenomenon" (p. 79). It is an ever-evolving transformation based on societal shifts, governmental action, familial environments, student/teacher actions, research findings, and other factors beyond the normal scope of control.

Effective principals understand their mission, chart the course, and navigate with an unwavering passion, vision, and courage, repelling negative energy. Dunklee (1999) believes "In almost a literal sense, the principalship is a moving, dynamic occupation" and "Managing the daily operation of a school while providing the leadership necessary to guide the school to educational excellence is an extremely complex task in an extremely complex organizational environment" (p. xii). Effective principals have a "whatever it takes" attitude and believe, whether expressed or concealed, that "failure is not an option" and that "excellence is the expectation."

SCHOOLS DESERVE EFFECTIVE PRINCIPALS

About a month after being hired as a central office administrator in a new district, I was delivering a professional development session for principals entitled "The Principalship: My Critically Reflective Perception through Blended Leadership Theory and Practice." The audience included the district's principals and assistant principals, along with other district-level employees, and the seventy-five-year-old superintendent of schools with fifty years of educational experience and the respected wisdom of a sage. This was my first public speaking engagement within the new district and from the new post.

The general purpose of the motivational session was to share experiences as a principal, along with fundamental beliefs about the principalship for inspiration at the beginning of the upcoming school year. About five minutes into the presentation, I stated, "The job of the principal is the most difficult position in the school system as far as I know it, but offers a great opportunity for direct influence." Since addressing a group of practicing principals and a group of former principals, it seemed like a *safe* statement. Wrong! The superintendent stopped the presentation, took off his glasses, and boldly said "I disagree."

A cold silence fell over the room and time appeared to be frozen at that moment. The superintendent said, "I believe the classroom teacher has the hardest job in the district." Standing before scores of professional educators as the new guy on the job, faced with this dilemma, the choice was to embrace the new enlightening as instructed by the superintendent or stand firm in my belief.

Realizing the possibility of career suicide, I respectfully (and publically) disagreed with my new boss by telling him, "The classroom teacher is the most important contributor to the academic progress of individual children and is where the actual rubber meets the road. But the level of responsibility placed on the principal from numerous stakeholders to achieve desired results form the basis of that opinion." He continued with, "Well, you're wrong."

After completion of the presentation, the superintendent approached and said, "Very good job—I'm impressed." The aforementioned staredown, which felt like a scene from an old western film, proved advantageous for authentic relationships with the principals of the district as they recognized my willingness to stand for the *principle* of the *principal* despite the calling to surrender. I felt strongly then and remain committed to the idea that effective principals are a necessity for healthy school cultures and significant academic achievements.

From a research base, there is a strong correlation between an effective principal and school improvement. Fullan (2001) wrote: "I know of no improving school that doesn't have a principal who is good at leading improvement" (p. 141). Sammons (1999), as cited in Fullan (2001), continued that "Almost every single study of school effectiveness has shown both primary and secondary leadership to be a key factor" (p. 141).

Additionally, Protheroe (2005) believes that "Leadership is the key to successfully navigating change" (p. 54). Roland Barth, author of *Improving Schools from Within* (1990), validates the import of school principals with "Show me a good school, and I'll show you a good principal" (p. 64). It has been demonstrated that improving schools and meeting school performance demands require strong school principals.

With the dynamics of society becoming increasingly complex, and under the assertion that schools are microcosms of the larger societal context, the need for effective leadership is fundamental to navigating the murkiness of change. Schools lacking proper principal leadership are doomed to a fate of underperformance or, at best, status-quo mediocrity. In emergency medical situations, few would settle for *adequate doctors* when lives are endangered; likewise, stakeholders should not accept *adequate principals.*

The children who grace school hallways will gradually become members of society at large and those children, as well as our society as a whole, deserve principals committed to ensuring academic achievement within a humanistic, democratic environment. While the greatest hope for an individual student's one-year achievement is found within the classroom teacher, the greatest hope for a host of students is found within the caring heart, exercised brain, and crafty hands of a skilled school principal.

SHIFTING PARADIGMS OF LEADERSHIP

The school accountability movement requires a new way of thinking and leading. This has created some confusion among school principals and the publics they serve. Wiseman (2005) suggested that "American principals are in peril" of becoming "victims of the growing accountability policies in the United States" (p. vii).

To succeed, and avoid school performance failure in the era of accountability, principals must establish new mindsets. Wheatley (1999) encourages her readers to "relinquish most of what we have cherished" to "see the world anew" (p. 7). The industrial-age paradigm of schools as mechanist machines and principals as commanding and controlling managers must cease for organizations of the twenty-first century to thrive.

Few people want *bosses* anymore; on the contrary, people want *leaders* who are values-driven, authentic, competent, and effective. Wheatley (2000) writes "Amid all the evidence that our world is radically changing, we cling to what has worked in the past" (p. 339). These traditionally held beliefs of schools and practices by their leaders stymie schooling and leadership's full realization of possibility. America can do better.

People often fall prisoner to their existing paradigms. In the *Republic*, Plato wrote of being captive to one's own mindset. Bloom (1968) presents Plato's "Allegory of the Cave" in his book, *The Republic of Plato*. The "Allegory of the Cave" provides a metaphor for the shackles of traditional management. In the "Allegory of the Cave," prisoners are held captive in a cave, facing the inward wall. A small fire casts light and shadows along the back wall of the cave, creating a reality for the captives. Finally, one of the captives is allowed to explore the outside world and realizes his previous reality was not truth. Instead, a new reality and truth existed.

Much like the captive prior to his freedom, traditional management practices form a reality for many school principals, even in the accountability era. Regarding the problems of traditional management, Wheatley (1999) believes "No problem can be solved from the same consciousness that created it" (p. 7). Douglas (2003) found "New leadership skills and behaviors are necessary" for organizations to thrive in today's environment (p. 6).

German sociologist Ferdinand Tönnies categorized two distinct sociological categories relevant to traditional management versus leadership. Tönnies introduced *gesellschaft* and *gemeinschaft* as opposing types of human association (Tönnies, 2002).

In a *gesellschaft* organization, strict hierarchical positions are known and maintained. Common goals are not shared and achieved because the greater good of the organization fails to supersede self-interests of individuals. Sergiovanni (1996) believes the "modern corporation is an example of *gesellschaft*" (p. 49).

On the contrary, *gemeinschaft* organizations hold a shared set of beliefs. Individuals within the organization lay aside their personal self-interests for the good of the organization they serve. A strong communal bond allows for powerful relationships and positive results. Sergiovanni (1996) added, "*Gemeinschaft* conceptions of schooling fit the developmental needs of students better, and are more likely to result in schools becoming more productive learning environments for students" (p. 186).

To move our schools toward *gemeinschaft*, traditional management must be replaced through a renewal of leadership. Looking into the future, Conley (1991) stated, "Principals in 2020 schools are serving as facilitators and developers, rather than bosses" (p. 38). Wiseman (2005) adds, "Good principals are not the 'chief' or the 'president'" of their schools, but instead are the "lifeblood" and the "oil that greases the wheel" (p. 36).

Sergiovanni (1995) insists, "Under conditions that require extraordinary commitment and performance, a great deal is at stake in developing a new and better-fitting theory" for leadership (p. 60). The constructs of this book, hopefully, will present a clear and present response for a principalship theory that can succeed in today's environment.

RESPONSIBILITY OF THE PRINCIPAL

When considering the new responsibilities of the principalship, a line from the movie *Spiderman* seems appropriate. Uncle Ben told young Peter Parker, "With great power comes great responsibility" (Ziskin and Arad, 2002). This line was undoubtedly adapted from President Franklin Delano Roosevelt's speech text, which stated, "Today we have learned in the agony of war that great power involves great responsibility." Furthermore, through historical tracking, President Roosevelt's words may have been inspired from Biblical text when Jesus Christ said, "To whom much has been given, much will be expected." Principals, through being chosen for their formal post, carry a heavy load of responsibility.

The realization of responsibility can be intimidating for the principal, but it is a necessity. Immediate responsibility for individual campuses falls upon the shoulders, whether thin or broad, of the school's principal. Overwhelmingly, educators want what is best for students—based, of course, on personal belief systems. The differences, however, lie within an educator's personal understanding of the word *best*, and professional demeanors are shaped by values and experiences.

One can envision the principal leading with an ethic of care for the students by wrapping them in services and support from the surrounding stakeholders. One can see the principal compounding true democracy and indoctrinating this ideal by involving all stakeholders in students' lives. One can see the principal supporting social justice in schools where students are provided an excellent education and are held accountable for their actions through both negative and positive consequences. One can see the principal expecting the best from students and demanding they quest for personal excellence.

If principals are satisfied with society outside of their school walls, then one can expect a similar or deteriorated micro-society within those walls. On the contrary, principals have a unique opportunity to change lives. Principals change lives through policy, principals change lives through expectations, principals change lives through relationships. In short, principals change lives because they have the ability to do so.

The question becomes, do principals change lives in a *positive* way? Do principals change lives through *democratic* policy? Do principals change lives through *high* expectations? Do principals change lives through *authentic* relationships? Do principals use positional authority as a license to empower all within their contact to become more fully human, more aware of the needs of others, and more productive citizens? For effective principals, the answer is a resounding *yes*.

Students within schools, in general and without check, are mirror images of our society. Our present society is one that includes many ills, including the destruction of previously universally accepted values. Current American society does not successfully promote positive attributes such as hard work, ingenuity, compassion, dependability, accountability, social justice, an ethic of care, respect, wholesomeness, or humility. Proper schools can change that.

Our democratic quest, in America, should not be taken for granted; instead, schools must cultivate and nurture democratic practices. Without hesitations, senses of perceptiveness and awareness must be built into students. Unfortunately, the present model of schooling places society at the top of an inverted pyramid pushing down on families, schools, and students. Instead of our schools being enslaved to the pervasive cultural and societal ills, principals should stand strong in creating campus environments of their antithesis. Schools, and their principals, shall work from a foundation that places students at the base of all considerations and decisions.

If students could be transformed into believing and practicing positive attributes, the entire school could shift. If schools could shift, families serviced by the school would shift. If schools can shift families, surely those families could shift society. For this to happen, creative and capable principals must emerge from the ashes. The work of the effective principal is both important for impact and hopeful as a new day's dawn.

INTERSTATE SCHOOL LEADERS LICENSURE CONSORTIUM (ISLLC)

As mentioned, today's school principal operates within a system of ever-increasing complexities, influenced by the breakdown of the nuclear family, frequent paradigm shifts within society, and an increased responsibility to perform in an era of educational accountability. Blaydes (2004) affirms, "The role of the principal has changed significantly in the past few years as a result of the impact of high-stakes accountability" (p. 3).

To overcome these challenges, principals benefit from embracing actions that blur research and theory into everyday practice, forming an effective praxis of educational leadership. Furthermore, the caring and committed principal develops a set of specific skills, enabling greater success in overcoming pressing challenges.

Presently, principals throughout the nation are guided by a set of six professional standards issued by the National Policy Board of Education Administration (NPBEA). The core competencies are known as the ISLLC standards of educational administration. These six specified performance standards are grounded in valid and reliable research and have grown in importance over the last decade.

The ISLLC standards have been most influential in moving educational leadership forward (Maxcy 2002). These standards seek to illuminate an operational framework and provide job clarity for the educational leader, including the school principal. All principal practices should find alignment, either directly or indirectly, within the ISLLC standards. Principals who satisfy each of the ISLLC standards should be considered as highly effective principals within their field. The six ISLLC Standards are:

Visionary Leadership. Educational leaders promote the success of every student by facilitating the development, articulation, implementation, and stewardship of a vision of learning that is shared and supported by all stakeholders.

Instructional Leadership. Educational leaders promote the success of every student by advocating, nurturing, and sustaining a school culture and instructional program conducive to student learning and staff professional growth.

Organizational Leadership. Educational leaders promote the success of every student by ensuring management of the organization, operation, and resources for a safe, efficient, and effective learning environment.

Collaborative Leadership. Educational leaders promote the success of every student by collaborating with faculty and community members, responding to diverse community interests and needs, and mobilizing community resources.

Ethical Leadership. Educational leaders promote the success of every student by acting with integrity, fairness, and in an ethical manner.

Political Leadership. Educational leaders promote the success of every student by understanding, responding to, and influencing the political, social, economic, legal, and cultural context.

INTRODUCING A CONSTRUCT

The ISLLC standards provide an outstanding framework for principals to situate their professional practice to ensure their leadership provides for a healthy, high-achieving school. To personally implement the standards, principals must approach each standard from a functional construct. In other words, principals must find ways to make internal sense of the standards and project those standards into action which maximizes their intended effectiveness. The leadership construct equates to a personal and authentic theory of leadership for each principal. Fullan (2008) argues that "Leaders need to develop and continually refine a good theory, defined as one that travels well in all kinds of situations" (p. 125).

The leadership construct, which forms the basis of the primary research for this book, is *Principal as Servant-Leader*. The ISLLC standards provide the operational and technical framework for the principalship, while the concept of servant-leadership provides the mode of relational application. The paradoxical idea of servant-leadership requires principals to place personal interests behind those of the school. In short, servant-leaders act as servants to the school and its stakeholders and, in turn, gain tremendous opportunities to move the school forward.

A LOOK AHEAD

The following chapter explicates servant-leadership from numerous dimensions, forming a basis of understanding for the concept and how, in general, its principles can guide implementation of the ISLLC standards.

Chapters 3 through 8 deconstruct each ISLLC standard through the lens of the servant-leader. Chapters 9 through 11 provide case studies of three highly effective school principals and illuminates their servant-leader characteristics. Conclusions are provided in the final chapter, along with a motivational charge to those seeking to better understand the principalship, those planning to enter the principalship, and those currently practicing as school principals.

TWO

Servant Leadership

Life is a place of service. Joy can be real only if people look upon their life as a service and have a definite object in life outside themselves and their personal happiness. — Leo Tolstoy

LEADING THROUGH LIFE'S STORMS

During the previous thirty-two years, Wayne Warner had weathered many storms as the principal of Chalmette High School in Louisiana. However, in 2005, his leadership would be tested in a way unlike anything he had ever experienced. Hurricane Katrina was a foe like no other.

When news of the approaching storm came, Warner's superintendent requested that he quickly convert the facility under his care from a school to a shelter. Chalmette High School, under Warner's direction, became a shelter of *last resort*. Opening the school as a shelter was, according to Warner, "a way to pay back to my community when it was in need because that's what school people do."

With little time to spare, the principal rallied his team and readied the school through preparation. They began accepting individuals and families concerned about the upcoming storm and provided for their immediate needs. Despite opportunities to flee, Warner made the conscious decision to stay with his school, and those under his care, throughout the storm.

As the powerful and brutal Hurricane Katrina made landfall, Warner recalls hearing the school's roof being ripped away, windows being blown out, and a hard rain coming into the building. Despite the loss of valuable electricity and having a school building in utter disrepair, the worst was yet to come.

15

By mid-morning, water was rising around the school. Seeing this, Warner, with the resolve of a veteran, directed the sick and disabled to be moved to a safe location. Within fifteen minutes, water was over five feet high and continuing to rise. Soon, water had reached an unprecedented level of eight feet deep surrounding the school. Community members began docking their boats atop the school's pavilion—this was an unbelievably unfortunate port. The Louisiana water was saturated with dangerous debris, oil, and wildlife, leading to primitive forms of communication and a basic quarantine within the shelter.

With circumstances dire, it became evident that present food and medical supplies were inadequate. The majority of stockpiled supplies were now six feet underwater and ruined. Making the situation worse was the uncertainty of exactly how long those located at Chalmette High School would be sheltered on site. Telecommunication was unavailable as towers had been rendered useless and other circuits were jammed. In an effort to ration for the unknown, Warner fed a bowl of dried Froot Loops and a half-cup of water each day to the evacuees at the Chalmette High School shelter. This rationing process continued for days.

Medically, the situation was grim. There were individuals needing ventilators, insulin, and dialysis to sustain their precious lives. One woman began giving birth in the middle of the gymnasium floor. On one occasion, an elderly gentleman told Warner he had twenty-four hours of oxygen remaining in his tank; then, came back and indicated he had made a mistake and only had two hours of oxygen left. Warner, as one can tell, was leading others through a crisis with a bravery inspired by the will to persevere.

The evacuees at the Chalmette Shelter had experienced a storm like no other and were forever changed. After weathering the storm's physical impact and its immediate aftermath, Warner finally led the evacuees to a Louisiana church further inland. From there, individuals and families planned for their uncertain futures after the storm, and Warner was there with them for selfless compassion and guidance.

Almost two months after Hurricane Katrina's devastating impact, Warner reopened school. Reminiscing, he shared, "It was the first day since Katrina that anybody smiled." On the first day of school, 334 students were in attendance and, within a month, 660 students were receiving an education in temporary buildings. Normalcy, to some degree, had thankfully returned to the Chalmette community.

Emotionally, Warner shared that rebuilding the school and the external community was, and continues to be, a difficult task. He is appreciative of people from throughout the country who gave gifts of money, goods, and services to provide for the needs of his school community. "Rebuilding our community is kind of like wresting a gorilla," Warner said. "You don't quit when you get tired; you quit when the gorilla gets tired and Katrina was like King Kong."

Things are gradually improving for Chalmette High School under Warner's continued leadership. When describing a major difference in relational culture, he proudly said, "Now, when people see each other, we hug; we don't shake hands." Tragedy intensifies relational community and, when properly led, schools become stronger after overcoming difficult odds. Warner doesn't believe he did anything especially significant or special during his service to his community both during and after Hurricane Katrina. In humble contrast, he shrugged and said, "That's what school people do."

NEW LEADERSHIP

The collective notions of the principalship and the actual work of individual principals must shift toward a blending of scholarship, service, and practice, forming a renewed praxis of educational leadership. The time has come for the era of *principal as boss* to be swept away and a new construct of *principal as servant-leader* to be ushered into the mindset of every aspiring principal, practicing principal, and principal-preparation specialist in America. The principalship, as a noble vocation, is a moral obligation that requires a humanistic approach to leading the organization toward collective purposes. When correctly practiced, the principalship carries beauty that balances the science of relevant knowledge and the art of graceful implementation.

More than any other educational group, principals have faced callings for change. These callings, however, have overwhelmingly been technical or programmatic instead of deeply rooted within a values structure for daily principal operation. These futile modifications have placed many principals in a leadership quagmire without a set of core beliefs to serve as a guide. Without a core construct from which to operate, principals prove to be reactive and nonpurposeful; however, principals with an identified belief system and congruency toward their values find peace with their work and significance with their impact.

Principals as servant-leaders place the needs of others and the health of the organization above personal desires. Allowing oneself to be a servant to individuals and the organization requires a principal to release power and become vulnerable as the organization itself gains power and grows strong and meaningful.

Throughout the 1900s, the structural view of organizations became a dominating and widely accepted force, extending into the realms of education. While structure is important toward school efficiency and effectiveness, a dictatorial structuralist will stifle creativity of faculty and students.

German economist and sociologist Max Weber viewed organizations as patriarchal, meaning they are dominated by a father figure with unlimited power. He coined the now-antiquated term *monocratic bureaucracy* to model an ideal organization maximizing rationality. Today, principalship openings throughout the nation are being filled with female educational leaders, ultimately smashing ideals of patriarchal dominance and any accepted *good 'ole boy* practices. The closer the demographics of the principalship mirror the demographics of our society as a whole, the more relevant the leadership should become.

While some schools have reached their goals through antiquated means, theorists are now considering new approaches for today's schools. Horn (2000) believes "There is a need for leaders who can build consensus and egalitarian community respectful of difference, rather than for managers who are grounded in industrial age theory and practice that promote the control and elimination of difference" (p. 1).

Again, old notions of *principals as bosses* must be replaced with renewed practice. The practices of managerial-type principals support the status-quo mediocrity and ultimate decay of the school. Sergiovanni (1995) believes traditional management practices may be overcome if "a new theory for the principalship" is developed, inspiring "extraordinary commitment and performance" (p. 45).

The challenges and demands of today's schools are different from the demands of the past. Quantz, Rogers, and Dantley (1991) stated, "American schools are in a period of confusion," continuing, "Traditional leadership theories are inadequate for meeting the present challenge" facing school principals (p. 96). Doing things the same way and expecting different results is evidence of insanity. Wheatley (1999) believes the "Science of the seventeenth century cannot explain what we are challenged by in the twenty-first century" (p. 161).

Our schools exist in a new world of exponential change. Servant-leadership is gaining currency as the construct of operation necessary to meet the myriad demands of the principalship. Hunter (2004) noted, "When it comes to leadership, many of us are saddled with old ideas and models" that may not be useful for leading in a "new and ever-changing world" (p. 57).

Servant-leadership veers from traditional practices of the principalship and replaces the leader's need for unlimited power and control with a leader's desire to authentically provide for the needs of the individuals under his/her care. It molds the principalship from a position that deals with people to a calling to genuinely lead others through service to their needs.

THE PARADOX OF SERVANT-LEADERSHIP

In his inaugural manifesto on servant-leadership, organizational leader, theorist, and writer Robert Greenleaf posed a question yet to be fully realized. Greenleaf (2001) asked, "Servant and leader—can these two roles be fused in one real person, in all levels of status or calling? If so, can that person live and be productive in the real world of the present?" (p. 21).

Strides, through research, have been made to answer Greenleaf's questions; however, the construct's relationship to school principals has lacked the full examination that it, and our schools, deserve. This emerging leadership construct, according to Leithwood and Montgomery (1986), as cited in Begley (2001), "implies a genuine kind of leadership—a hopeful, open-ended, visionary and creative response to social circumstances, as opposed to the more traditional dualistic portrayal of management and leadership practices" (p. 354).

Understanding the servant's ability to lead is also foundational to explaining the paradox. Greenleaf's idea of the servant as leader came to him from Hermann Hesse's *The Journey to the East* (1956). The story follows a band of men on a mythical journey. Leo, the lead character, traveled with the men as their servant, handling all the *small jobs* and providing the other men with their basic needs. In addition, Leo sustained the men with his songs and his unbreakable spirit.

The journey transpired wonderfully until Leo, their servant, disappeared from the group. With the absence of its servant, the group dismantles and abandoned its journey. The narrator, who was one of the men, later reflected on the journey, only to determine that Leo was more than their servant—he was "its guiding spirit, a great and noble leader" (Greenleaf 2002, 21). Many of the same characteristics displayed by Leo are required for servant-leadership in today's schools; however, these characteristics are not yet understood or appropriately communicated to those principals seeking a better way of leading.

SERVANT-LEADERSHIP PRAXIS

Principals seeking to become significant influences in the lives of stakeholders and in the overall success of schools must have an effective leadership praxis. In the context of the twenty-first-century principalship, a leadership praxis is the ability to understand, articulate, and implement valued research, theory, and values into the year-to-year, day-to-day, and moment-to-moment decisions of the school principal. A servant-leader's praxis appreciates the value of individuals and their contributions toward the overall health of the organization without favoritism.

As an obligation, principals as servant-leaders help create and improve schools. In turn, these schools function as healthy organizations consisting of, and for, the students, faculty, and community. Furthermore, principals as servant-leaders seek to employ operations that encourage a synergistic harmony of the organization and further advance schools toward overarching missions and a collective vision.

A personal feedback loop of reflection for practice keeps the principal as servant-leader well informed. Moreover, their current and future practices are, through a reciprocal relationship, advanced through new scholarship. The relationship of learning about leadership and seeking improved educational strategy is closely aligned to the daily practices of the principal. The praxis of a principal as servant-leader is one that is constantly seeking improvement immediately for the children under his or her care, faculty to be grown, and the larger society, both in the present and future.

Principals as servant-leaders gain direction through examination into French culture. A *criticalist bricoleur* is a French handyman who uses necessary tools included in his toolbox to complete the assigned task. These handymen are diagnosticians and understand the correct instrumentation for problem correction. Likewise, principals as servant-leaders must act using all means necessary, within legal and moral limits, to meet the needs of those they serve. Only with an informed praxis of knowledge and understanding do principals as servant-leaders have a complete scope of tactics and strategies to achieve desired results.

A SERVANT'S ATTITUDE

The mindset in which principals approach their daily work forms the attitude of their leadership. And, attitudes, as one knows, are highly contagious. With this understanding, it is fundamentally important that principals lead with the attitude of a servant, prompting and essentially acting as a catalyst for the reproduction of further servant-like behaviors throughout the campus. So, what does the attitude of a servant look like?

A principal as servant-leader approaches the day with a humble confidence and does whatever it takes, with no job too big and no task too small, to meet the personal needs of stakeholders as they advance the school toward its predetermined and collective purpose.

Through this mindset of humility, the principal as servant-leader sees no need to announce authority or power; instead, through confidence in one's abilities, the servant-leader shatters hierarchical and other vertical structures and becomes a contributing member of the school. There is no doubt, through the operational and anointed title of *principal*, that positional authority is understood. With this, there is no purposeful reason to announce or otherwise project a higher status than employees, students, or other stakeholders.

When principals cloak indicators of an advanced status or pedigree, stakeholders become more comfortable, which leads to flourished creativity and an improved school morale. Furthermore, the idea and practice of caring service is recognizable and assimilates into their paradigm of life.

The principal as servant-leader seeks an enhanced awareness of the school as a culture and as a functioning agency. Through this perceptiveness, the principal is cognizant of the school's *big picture* while empowering its people to be more, do more, and achieve more by providing emotional support, intellectual growth, and physical resources needed for success.

Functioning as a resilient servant, the principal is not forever deterred by any political, social, or financial impasse that might permanently sidetrack other organizations. As the principal boldly and courageously fosters the growth of teamwork within the school, individuals gain a feeling of greater self-worth, which benefits the whole.

SERVANT SYNOPSIS

Servant-leaders facilitate processes on their campuses to achieve a predetermined vision package with specific missions and goals. With an understanding that schools exist for a purpose, the principal as servant-leader approaches work, each day, with a sense of urgency and focus. Having an appropriately humanistic consciousness, principals as servant-leaders realize the value of individuals as worthy beings; however, they also appreciate the contributions of individuals toward doing the work of the organization.

Servant-leaders recognize the importance and value of others, build relationships, praise individuals, empower goodness, and, ultimately, evolve to heightened personal levels of success and an overall healthy organizational unit. By replacing selfishness with selflessness, principals as servant-leaders situate the needs of others and the organization ahead of greedy personal gains. Through these practices, principals as servant-leaders gain much respect and credibility. As hierarchical, political, and bureaucratic walls are broken down, the distributed power of the people is unleashed, resulting in increased organizational quality.

IMPLEMENTING THE ISLLC STANDARDS

The ISLLC standards for school administration are heavily grounded in research and are valuable guides for those seeking to become school principals and those seeking to become improved school principals. Principals who correctly implement the ISLLC standards and their underlying tenets will find success. For a greater likelihood of success, or even significance, principals should adopt the analogy of principal as servant-leader. Over the next chapters, the ISLLC standards will stand as the organizational framework. Within each chapter, the standards will be deconstructed from the lens of an effective principal as servant-leader.

THREE

Visionary Leadership

 If your actions inspire others to dream more, learn more, do more and become more, you are a leader. — John Quincy Adams

A CENTRAL PURPOSE

When Todd Purvis considered the principalship of Central City Academy, located in inner-city New Orleans, he knew the challenges were immense; however, he also visualized opportunities to positively shape lives of high-risk youth. For him, moving individual students forward through a values-based education outweighed any hesitation.

"When I arrived, I knew I had to get everyone on board with what needed to be done," Purvis said. "I had to build a strong school culture and I knew I had to leverage everyone so that we could achieve a mission for our school."

Central City Academy is a part of Louisiana's Recovery School District, the statewide system that assumes responsibility for schools deemed failing. The school, consisting of approximately four hundred students, has a configuration of fifth through eighth grades and is now operated by the Knowledge is Power Program (KIPP), a network of open-enrollment, college-preparatory schools throughout the United States.

At present, 95 percent of the students receive free or reduced lunch, 99 percent are African American, and 10 percent of the population has been identified in need of special-education services. With demographics typical of inner-city youth, Central City certainly has challenges to overcome. "One of my primary goals was to communicate the mission and values, to benchmark toward success, and to provide everyone the support they needed to meet our goals," Purvis shared.

The vision package for the school, facilitated by Purvis as the school's leader, is clearly designed, constantly communicated, and embedded in actions, and progress is monitored to ensure success. It includes values, a mission statement, and specific goals to achieve. With this cohesive vision package, Central City has made tremendous strides in numerous areas. "Our school culture is so strong," Purvis added. "We have a sense of urgency and purpose that makes our school truly unique."

The worthy and accepted values of the school are excellence, family, grit, integrity, teamwork, and zest. In its mission, Central City is dedicated to preparing students for success beyond middle and high school. In visionary fashion, the purpose of the school is to prepare students for college success, even though their students are five to eight years away from even enrolling at a university. In fact, the mission statement for the school reads, "to prepare all kids with the academic skills and character traits to excel in college."

Mission statement

Related to specific goals, Central City expects to increase its state-assigned school performance score, keep students on a college preparatory track, instill character skills based on values within the students, and have 100 percent of its students pass coursework and state testing.

"We are constantly reflecting to make sure that everyone in the building and everything we do aligns to our values and mission," Purvis communicated. "We do constant messaging of the vision to everyone, we spend professional development time on the values and goals, and we frequently benchmark on our goals."

In terms of academic accountability, Central City has shown substantial improvement. In two years, and with the focused support of Purvis, the school has improved its accountability score by approximately 30 percent. At present, the school performance score of Central City Academy is approximately 40 percent higher than schools with a similar configuration in the same geographical area.

As one can easily notice, Central City Academy is making significant strides toward improving the present and future lives of students while improving as an organization. No doubt, through the vision and determination of Principal Purvis, Central City has benefitted from a calculated, explicit, and shared vision package as the school's purpose.

In consideration of the success of Central City, the words of Wheatley (1999) seem especially relevant. She wrote, "The music comes from something we cannot direct, from a unified whole created among the players—a relationship holism that transcends separateness. In the end, when it works, we sit back, amazed and grateful" (p. 87).

STANDARD #1

An educational leader promotes the success of every student by facilitating the development, articulation, implementation, and stewardship of a vision of learning that is shared and supported by all stakeholders.

A VISION PACKAGE

Many schools throughout the United States have school for the sake of having school. One might ask, *What does that mean?* This indicates that individuals, both students and employees, arrive at a building every morning, go through their days in isolation, and go home when the final bell sounds with little to no consideration of an organizational unit's collective purpose. Even schools showing promise in certain areas, departments, or with certain initiatives, will often, when given further review, find their school is actually *having school for the sake of having school.*

In these buildings, school provides a means of employment for some, childcare for parents, and produces some positive results including relative amounts of learning and other successes. However, schools meeting the above description are not maximizing their possibilities for significance in the lives of all stakeholders. Unfortunately and sadly, the average American school fits, to some degree, within this context.

The school principal, more than any other individual, holds the greatest potential to reculture a school with unity and collective purpose. Duffy (2003) believed that "Redesigning whole systems is a daunting task that requires a special breed of leader" (p. 3). That "breed" of extraordinary principal is the servant-leader with foresight and recognition of the need for a healthy and purposeful school. Beyond recognition, the effective principal facilitates a process of planning, implementation, and refinement to provide commonality and vigor to the school.

School principals understand their role as one of service to the future of both the students and health of the organization. An effective leader considers conditions beyond the present to a more hopeful and democratic tomorrow.

Beyond this visualization, these principals ensure conditions conducive to achievement. DeSpain (2000) found that leadership is "an imperfect art practiced by those who lead in which the leader defines reality for his or her followers while creating and nurturing a vision of a new, better reality to come," and this described leader "subsequently nurtures and serves the organization, the followers, and the dreams of the vision as all seek to attain the new reality" (p. ix). Furthermore, principals as servant-leaders possess humble confidence through a belief that they can improve the school, make a difference, and improve the lives of individuals.

Setting a tone of organizational purpose is vital for school success. Boyer (1995) found that "A school community is, first, a purposeful place, with a clear and vital mission," and "Research reveals that when school purposes are well defined and energetically pursued, student performance will improve" (p. 18).

This chapter provides, in sequence, a guide for bringing meaning and purpose to the school organization through a collective vision package. It provides insight on the development of a school purpose and creates a real response to ineffective and inefficient organizational structures that lack the visionary requirements for a school to be both successful and significant.

As read, a *vision statement* is not developed; instead, a sequence is provided to articulate and implement organizational purpose which, when combined, forms an overall vision for the school led by a principal as servant-leader. The organization's values, mission statement, and goals are the required elements of a school's vision package.

Needs Assessment

Schools benefit from principals conducting needs assessments of schools. The idea of conducting a needs assessment in a school, for some reason, does not receive much currency in the field of educational research. It is, however, a process of inquiry nurtured within a school that is seeking transparency and growth for the benefit of all stakeholders.

Some states and districts have specific instruments prescribed for use. In the absence of a mandated instrument, a simple tool can be created to provide valuable information and form a starting point or guide a refinement process. There are two primary categories of the needs assessment: empirical data and perceptual data.

The needs assessment includes empirical data related to coursework and standardized testing success by content area, attendance, behavioral referral numbers, promotion/graduation rates, and any other statistic important to the specific school. This data can be gathered by the principal and/or administrative team, considering confidential and sensitive content is involved.

Perceptual data that outlines the *feelings* or *attitudes* of the school's stakeholders is gathered as well. When gathering perceptual data, it is imperative that participants are assured a safe environment in which to freely provide their opinions. This can be done through assuring confidentiality, anonymity, and an overall proper protocol for the data collection. Some might believe the opinions of students, faculty, parents, and community members are erroneous and are based on limited information without the full range of facts. Perception is reality, and it is an issue principals must address if the perception is negative.

Once information is collected, the principal can determine areas of school strengths and concerns that need immediate, corrective attention. Having this information sets a baseline for statistical improvement. And, as an overarching vision, principals as servant-leaders seek to create a healthy school environment for all stakeholders in order to advance the collective and purposeful organization toward improvement.

Values Clarification

Individuals operate from an internal set of core values that drives their decision-making process and informs their practice. These demonstrated values form the basis of one's character. Principals as servant-leaders hold an internal values structure that places the good of individuals and the organization they serve above selfish interests in authentic form. Within the organization, principals as servant-leaders seek to provide necessary direction, guidance, resources, and skills to move the school closer toward aligning actions with espoused values.

A school that is appropriately values-based has a greater probability of values-achievement. In order to successfully operate from predetermined values, the school organization must first determine the values that it cherishes and holds dear. From these held and practiced values, the character of the school is defined.

A team is organized to clarify the specific positive values the school desires to communicate and practice. As a contributing member of the team, the principal assumes the role of facilitator of the process. The protocol for selecting the values of the school will vary from school to school; however, by the end of the process, a set of core values are universally accepted by the committee as a whole.

Some popular and worthy values, for example, are care, cooperation, democracy, excellence, hope, and loyalty. These are examples and may or may not reflect the most important values desired by a specific school. The five to ten most important values selected by the team serve as an absolutely necessary set of operational beliefs for the school. The values, once accepted, are not compromised, and every decision made at the school is based upon achieving these values. From these values, a school develops its mission statement.

[handwritten margin note: Crafting a Mission Statement]

Mission Statement

When one considers a military force undertaking a mission, thoughts are elicited of a specific job or tasking that must be completed. We believe the mission is the fundamental purpose; it is the central desired outcome of the time and resources invested. School principals as servant-leaders adopt a similar mindset for the school's mission and communicate that mission through a living statement.

The mission statement is the overarching purpose for the school and provides an organizing mission to be achieved. There is a common misconception that *mottos* or *slogans* are viable substitutes for a mission. This misconception has caused problematic realities of organizing a school toward an overarching purpose. Although it is acceptable for schools to adopt cute or clever mottos or slogans, it is not acceptable for this nonholistic verbiage to be considered as a comprehensive, stand-alone outcome of the school.

Again, a team is enlisted for this process. This team consists of members apart from those stakeholders who determined the values of the school. In the creation of a mission statement, several factors are considered. A haphazard approach is not taken to determine the overarching purpose of the school. Instead, the mission's basis is an understanding of the statistical and perceptual data collected from the needs assessment and the beliefs selected by the team through the values-clarification process. These items form the basis for the content of the mission. Furthermore, as an obligation, the principal as servant-leader ensures, through contribution to the mission-statement team, a servant-oriented slant that is hopeful of an optimistic future.

Once the team determines the specific content of the statement, there is a period of brainstorming, creating interplay of word structures. The team considers ways to articulate an aesthetic sentence that communicates needs, values, service, and hope while comprehensively developing an overarching and holistic purpose for the organization. The mission statement clearly conveys the priority of the school as a functioning organization. The mission statement extends beyond a one-year product; instead, the school's mission provides a visionary articulation that sets the organizational purpose for years to come.

Goals

After a mission statement is adopted, a goal-setting team is created to establish the school's specific goals for the year. This team, again, consists of a new set of members. The rationale for having three different teams for values clarification, mission-statement development, and goal setting is to engage as many stakeholders as possible and provide them with direct ownership of the structure being created. While the mission of the school lasts for multiple years, school goals are reviewed yearly and altered, changed, and/or refined as needed for the benefit of the individual stakeholders and the school as an organizational, purposeful unit.

The goal-setting team gives careful consideration to the school's newly adopted mission statement and determines the goals the school will establish for achieving progress toward that mission. The goals are reflective of the school's purpose as established through the mission and directed through the values.

Based on school configuration and other site-specific needs, in concert *Goals* with the mission statement, the goals should be concrete and measurable. Some reasonable goals, for example, would be 95-percent attendance, a ↑ 10-percent reduction in behavior referrals, a 5-percent increase in English *examples* proficiency on a standardized test, three new community-service pro- ↓ jects, or a 100-percent student graduation/promotion rate.

The determined goals, either directly or indirectly, advance the school toward reaching its mission. Furthermore, the goals must be measurable, realistically attainable through diligence, and worthwhile toward creating a more democratically intelligent citizenry, both within the context of the school and into their futures. Immediately, however, plans must be developed to achieve each goal.

Plans for Action (PfAs)

Sequentially, the next step in a school's visionary process involves creating Plans for Action (PfAs) to meet each of the established goals. The semantics of Plans *for* Action is important because *for* places emphasis on having active responses prepared to meet goals. Instead of a sedentary plan, the plans are dynamic and involve commitment, not simply compliance, from all stakeholders. PfAs are developed based upon the specific goals with team members selected in a common sense manner. For example, team members for a numeracy-improvement goal would probably differ from the members for a behavioral-achievement goal.

PfAs outline detailed procedures for achieving each goal. Serving as the school's playbook for systematically and methodically making the goals become a reality, PfAs are necessary for schools interested in being purposeful and not whimsically disorganized and chaotic.

The PfAs include the target goal, specific initiatives for reaching the goal, responsible individuals, dates and methods for progress monitoring, and other pertinent information with the target goal in mind. As a rule, PfAs should be more specific and concrete rather than abstract. Furthermore, details and clarity are very important when considering PfAs.

Progress Monitoring

With the school's mission, goals, and PfAs developed, it is then beneficial to establish dates and measures for monitoring progress toward goal attainment. The process of progress monitoring requires basic status checks on multiple occasions throughout the school year to determine if the school is on track toward meeting the goals.

Common checkpoints for progress monitoring are monthly, quarterly, or grading-period based. The checkpoint dates are based on the goal in question and are pragmatically determined. A semester-based progress monitoring of goals is not productive as it limits response or intervention time if results are not at desired levels.

Progress monitoring of goals is directly related to achieving them. If, for example, a school has a goal of reading nine thousand books for the school year, progress monitoring might occur monthly. Assuming a nine-month academic year, the school's students should have read one thousand books the first month, two thousand books after the second month, and so on. If it is determined that the current pacing will not provide goal attainment, an intervention to shore the deficit and set the school back on chart before year's end has time to be implemented.

This might require the principal as servant-leader to provide additional resources, professional development, or other incentives to ameliorate any deficits. If intervention or augmentation is necessary, the PfAs team reviews its document and makes needed revisions within the school year. It takes this type of systemic and calculated dedication and awareness from a school's principal to ensure success of the goals and mission.

Progress monitoring, as mentioned, is specific to the individual goals. Because goals are quantifiable, they can be mathematically progress monitored. Progress-monitoring results are recorded and filed for future decisions and goal setting. Although this is a time-consuming process, it is imperative to heightened levels of success.

Communicating the Vision

As the school's chief communicator, the principal has the responsibility to transmit the school's vision to all stakeholders. A centrality of language exists among all stakeholders, signifying an understanding and appreciation of the vision.

Principals utilize the vision to initiate activities and programming designed to achieve great success. Fullan (2001) stated that "The main problem is not the absence of innovation in schools, but rather the presence of too many disconnected, episodic, fragmented, superficially adorned projects" (p. 21). Principals must be servants to the mission and not allow external and nonfocused activity to negatively impact the school's purpose.

The school's faculty and staff is the first grouping of stakeholders to receive the comprehensive vision package, inclusive of mission, goals, and PfAs. This meeting happens before the beginning of the school year, ensuring that a lucid presence is made for the vision, that clarifications of the vision package are made, and that all questions are answered. The principal as servant-leader to the vision facilitates this dialogue and provides an expectation of individual and collective accountability toward the vision.

Furthermore, before students enter the building for the year, the vision package is aesthetically displayed through visual representations.

Appropriate signage is displayed at crucial, high-traffic locations throughout the building to articulate the vision. Although frugality is a consideration for every American school, it is vitally important to have the mission statement posted throughout the school with prominence and reverence.

Suggestions include large, professionally designed and framed signage throughout the school halls. Although this can be relatively expensive, a monetary value cannot be given to providing and articulating the overarching purpose of the organization. In presentation of the goals throughout the school, more consideration is given to expense. Because goals change from year to year, a principal determines practical and economical ways to project these throughout the building.

During the first opportunity to speak to the student body and/or parents, the principal boldly presents the vision package to all available stakeholders. With the presence and command of a skilled orator seeking to meet the audience on common ground, the principal should share "This is what we're going to do" and "This is how we're going to do it." During this presentation, the principal seeks to build consensus and support for the vision package and enlist the stakeholders as active supporters and contributors to the cause. Furthermore, the principal offers him or herself as a servant to the cause with a "whatever it takes" attitude.

The principal views communication of the vision package not in terms of a single event, but instead, sees it as an ongoing process of dialogue with all stakeholders. The principal utilizes both planned and spontaneous opportunities for maintaining a focus on the ultimate vision. Using all available forums such as open houses, back-to-school nights, parent conferences, and holiday programs, the principal capitalizes on having an audience to hear the message.

Jim

Furthermore, principals can communicate the mission and goals on a daily basis to all students by allotting a few minutes at the beginning of every school day for announcements, celebrations, democratic rituals, and vision focus. This is most effective in the form of a daily morning assembly. Communication of the vision package to all involved parties *Weekly Newsletters* through electronic sources and networks is especially important and convenient in this technological age.

Every school stakeholder should be able to articulate the vision package of the mission and goals. The PfAs are internal documents utilized by the administration, faculty, and staff and are not to be provided, in detail, to all stakeholders. The PfAs are disseminated on a "need-to-know" basis. The more frequent the vision package is communicated, the better the end results. Then, through an understanding of the vision package, there is a greater chance of actual vision attainment, consisting of reaching the mission and achieving the goals as all stakeholders operate from the appropriate and accepted values structure.

Celebrations

One of the most joyous times for a school principal and productive occasions for improving school culture and morale is through the celebration of success. All achieved goals should be celebrated and all stakeholders congratulated for their combined efforts in a successful attainment. As servants of both stakeholders and the organization, principals realize there is no success too small to celebrate.

With a myriad of negative factors attempting to sabotage the schooling processes and the attitudes of its stakeholders, celebrations of success are simple and often inexpensive methods for rewarding behavior leading to goal achievement. Also, celebrations of success set the stage for future goals. When faculty and students experience success, and are recognized and rewarded for it, more success is fostered. It also advances the school's culture to one where excellence is the expectation.

Celebrations of success at schools do not require extravagant measures. In contrast, students and faculty are often quite content with inexpensive measures when provided with authentic, genuine appreciation. There is typically capacity within the school to plan and implement celebrations of success in creative ways for the school community to enjoy and become saturated in the laurels of accomplishment.

Reflection and Refinement

As a source of continuous improvement, principals as servant-leaders are willing to critically reflect on the organization's vision package and make needed refinements for the betterment of the school. Principals seeking refinement first engage in reflective endeavors to facilitate the process. The reflective movement comes from one's internal determinations of the organizational progress toward a vision; however, a principal as servant-leader allows for open vulnerability and seeks the thoughts and opinions of all stakeholders, a sign of leadership courage and confidence.

A principal as servant-leader creates an expectation of reflection on and of practice. York-Barr, Sommers, Ghere, and Montie (2006) found "The ultimate goal of school-wide reflective practices is continuous improvement of organizational, team, and individual practices in order to increase student learning," and continued by stating that "Increased student learning requires coherence and continuity in the educational experience for students, which requires strong connections among educators throughout the school" (p. 201). The results of reflection are overwhelmingly positive in consideration of its potential to improve organizational effectiveness and efficiency.

This is not the final step in the process of visionary leadership; instead, reflection and refinement are a vital component of a cyclical process of questing toward the vision. It is the responsibility of the principal as servant-leader to selflessly give of self for the advancement of the school. The organizational health of the school is fundamentally important to the principal as a servant-leader seeking to implement a vision of both success and significance for all stakeholders of the school.

FOUR

Instructional Leadership

Unless pains are taken to see that genuine and thorough transmission takes place, the most civilized group will relapse into barbarism and then into savagery. —John Dewey

QUALITY INSTRUCTION; SIGNIFICANT GAINS

Virtually hidden in the heart of Louisiana's Cajun culture, where the zydeco music is bold and the gumbo is fresh, is a gem of an educational institution. The school, Eunice Elementary, serves a melting pot of students and has sustained tremendous school-performance growth.

The principal, Irma Trosclair, deconstructs any notion of servant-leaders being passive; instead, in terms of student learning, Trosclair is quite authoritative in her approach as a servant to student learning. "Doing what is best for students is our only option," said Trosclair. "I understand and clearly communicate the urgency in what we do because this is life or death for young people."

Eunice Elementary is making significant academic progress, as monitored by an ambitious Louisiana accountability protocol. Over the past few years, the school has seen an approximate 47-percent gain in school performance data. The high standards of learning and implementation of effective programming and practices are vital to Trosclair's leadership style. As a result of its accomplishments, the school has been named a National Blue Ribbon School—a prestigious honor.

"When I became principal, instruction seemed to be random with no evident focus or driving force," shared Trosclair. "Those days of a hit-and-miss approach are gone because our new instruction is specific, focused, well thought out, and driven by data." At Eunice Elementary, teachers focus on strategically aligning their instructional practices with the curriculum. Furthermore, they provide extensions for above and on-level students while providing tailored interventions in core content areas for struggling students.

As a collaborative team, they meet regularly to review individual performance data to make instructional decisions for each student. In planning for success, Trosclair designed faculty professional development in consideration of weak areas in student data.

"I offer support to teachers because I know they are the ones doing the important work," voiced Trosclair. "I constantly analyze, breakdown data, and research to give teachers the information they need so that together we can make sound decisions for our children." Over her nine years as principal, improving the instructional culture has been a test of Trosclair's patience. She has been both committed and laser focused with initiatives and expectations to improve student learning. Trosclair has focused her instructional leadership, in calculative form, on one or two areas each year. Over time, the entire instructional atmosphere has shifted in a positive way.

"We have built a solid educational program because there is consistency and simplicity in what we do," Trosclair said. "Although our techniques are simple in nature, they are intensive in our efforts to continuously improve our program."

The students at Eunice Elementary, in a regionally specific Cajun culture, are afforded the right to a quality education. Within the walls of their campus, they are provided core knowledge that prepares them for future schooling success and competency to ultimately compete in a global economy.

STANDARD #2

An educational leader promotes the success of every student by advocating, nurturing, and sustaining a school culture and instructional program conducive to student learning and staff professional growth.

The Reason Schools Exist

From a democratic, economical, and social standpoint, schools exist for learning to materialize with students. There is commonality in a desire for schooling to enhance student understanding of themselves, their futures, and their world with hopes of maturation into contributing, creative, and generally productive members of our American citizenry.

Although principals have varied and complex duties throughout their work, the most fundamental reason for their existence is the responsibility of ensuring student learning. Without a doubt, students benefit from principals who are passionate servants to maximizing student learning.

These principals as servant-leaders are instructionally competent, energetic, and driven toward heightened levels of student learning and achievement. They have committed themselves to the cause of providing valuable learning opportunities for the students under their care.

Recent polling suggests less than one-fifth of the average principal's day is dedicated to instructional leadership. Given prescribed learning as the primary function of a school, it is both irresponsible and negligent that principals, in general, are not giving instruction due consideration in their daily schedules.

Time is the most valuable commodity and acts as the currency for each day's work. When little time is afforded toward explicitly improving instruction, principals are not serving the primary function of their role as instructional leaders. In essence, the public's investment in the principal is not paying reasonable dividends in the area of student learning.

While it is challenging, due to the complexity of the job, principals as servant-leaders prioritize learning and ensure that a controlling majority of their day, as a percentage, is invested into instructional leadership. The responsibility of enhancing school-wide instructional quality, leading to increased student learning, resides within the school principal's willingness and ability to accept the challenge of instructional improvement.

Even with a newfound devotion to ensuring student learning, principals will not find a comprehensive definition of, or theory for, instructional leadership. Smith and Andrews (1989) noted that an effective principal is often labeled with phrases of description such as: "runs a tight ship," "keeps the parents at bay," "knows the district inside and out," and "keeps the building ship-shape" (p. 7).

However, imagery related specifically to instructional leadership, and a new mindset for a nonmanager principal, is more elusive. A responsibility of our current and future generation of principals is to form and refine a new mold of instructional leadership that can be clearly defined through words and actions.

A paradigm shift must be made in instructional relationships. Principals should move beyond a managerial view of instructional leadership that gives primary focus on teacher inputs with secondary attention given to student outputs. A more sensible, more appropriate, yet virtually unused concept is that which focuses attention on student outputs based on teacher inputs. Simply, the outcome of instruction is not a matter of what a teacher says or does. Instead, instruction is the sum of what students are able to say and do as a result of a teacher's effort.

Too often, especially with teacher observations, principals are evaluating the teacher based on what he or she is doing without consideration of student performance. A more fitting approach for a principal is observations that note student outcomes as a result of the teacher. Freire (1998) believed "There is, in fact, no teaching without learning . . . one requires the other" (p. 31). With this, we cannot view instruction as an isolated set of actions.

On the contrary, we must expand instruction's meaning to a continuous dynamic in which teachers facilitate constructive learning experiences for students in a safe and comfortable environment where learning and teaching have a reciprocal and mutually benefiting relationship.

At the school's instructional core lies a principal who is impeding, maintaining, or enhancing the overall instructional culture through a winning instructional attitude and comprehensive, effective, and technical programming. The desired principal is the latter, and, as a servant to the school's values, wages a war on ineffective instructional practices that prohibit the school from reaching its vision, mission, and goals.

Seeking the Vision

Every instructional decision shall seek to achieve the school's vision. Instructional programming is part of a specific Plan for Action (PfA) of the school. The PfA helps achieve a specific goal. The goal assists in reaching the mission for the school. These components are the body of the school's vision package.

To secure focused attention on an established vision, principals must ensure alignment between all instructional activity and the quest toward the vision. Principals become servants of the vision package and diligently navigate the vessel of the school toward the collectively shared vision. As a committed holder of a better tomorrow, the principal is responsible for prioritizing teaching and learning with the vision package forever in mind. This will, at times, require weeding of unaligned and sporadic thorns of instructional activity.

Challenging ineffective practices requires great courage and resolve from the principal, especially when these weeds are historically and traditionally rooted in the school's instructional culture. Courage, as needed, is not leadership without fear. In fact, fear of the unknown is actually an important stressor in the life of the school principal seeking to facilitate instructional change. Duffy (2003) wrote that "Being courageous means facing fear and doing what has to be done in spite of it" (p. 5).

Ineffective instructional practices are present, to varying degrees, in every school in America—this is a constant. The unknown, however, is the principal's willingness to confront and ability to ameliorate the instructional inadequacies within the school for the betterment of the student.

With a deeply embedded commitment to achieving the school's mission on behalf of all stakeholders, the principal finds solace in leading a charge of instructional improvement. As an oft-embattled protector and seeker of the vision, the principal finds clarity in purpose despite the prevalent challenges.

Dialogue of Constructive Experience

A considerable portion of the general population and educational community holds an erroneous belief about student learning. Their faulty belief is one that views the student as a sponge to be expanded with knowledge given by a teacher. This notion renders the student powerless to learn without a teacher. On the contrary, students and teachers are both active participants in the learning process through an exchange of dialogue in the form of activity, critical thinking, discussion, reading, writing, and other worthy exchanges.

As noted in a critically powerful sense, dialogue is more than simple conversation; instead, it is an energetic interplay guided by action and reflection within both the teacher and the student. Increasing student learning and overall student achievement does not require a secret code or key to unlock a mysterious box of treasure.

Schmoker (1999) insists that "Incremental, even dramatic, improvement is not only possible but probable under the right conditions that favor results" (p. 1). The *right conditions* are those environments in which a rich dialogue of constructivist experiences are present between teacher and student and where special attention is given to the vital elements of consistency, depth, and frequency.

The effective principal creates an academic environment where teachers are encouraged to be facilitators of learning and to maximize the impact of every moment they spend with students. A moment of instructional loss is a moment never to be regained. The work of the classroom teacher is too immense for idle discretionary time; instead, seeking the school's vision requires every moment to be purposefully utilized and filled with student learning experiences.

The principal serves by setting the expectation and assuring the implementation of "a comprehensive approach that allows for student construction of meaning while interacting with the content, the teacher, and other students" in every classroom (Marzano 2007, 2).

Establishing an expectation that each classroom be filled with constructive experiences of dialogue requires, foundationally, support from all teachers. In essence, the instructional faculty must realize the importance of educating students in this manner. This situation requires the principal to serve as a facilitator, either directly or indirectly, of adequate professional development of a constructivist pedagogy of educational experience.

The principal forges the path toward effective educational strategy and models for the faculty. Beyond a developed instructional skill set, principals require an ideological zest to improve the world. Principals cannot cloak a superficial passion for fulfilling life's purpose, they must love the teachers, and they cannot neglect the relational component of establishing an authentic dialogue of improved instructional practice.

Freire (1970) contended, "If I do not love the world, if I do not love life, if I do not love people, I cannot enter into dialogue" (p. 90). True communication, which is two-way between parties, is a requirement for developing appropriate educational practices within the school.

Also gaining currency is the idea of student opportunity to learn (OTL). In the specific sense of instruction, opportunity to learn gives deliberation to, for example, the teaching environment, pedagogy, and resources. Starratt (2003) argues that "If all students are to be held to the same standards . . . they must have equal access to high-quality instruction" (p. 298). Principals ensure the presence of resources intended to impact learning.

At the school level, primary principal consideration is given to equal allocation of resources to teachers, and to maintaining that all teachers perform at high levels where teachers receive appropriate professional development, and where teachers feel they are supported in their efforts to increase student learning. Furthermore, principals as servant-leaders recognize the importance of building leadership capacity within teachers to provide opportunity to learn within their individual classrooms.

Clarke (2005) believed, "Regardless of changes that principals plan and implement, teachers carry the banner forward to the objective" (p. 15). With all parties working together to create impactful opportunities to learn, positive outcomes in the school are exponentially multiplied. Duffy (2003) asserts these contributions from all stakeholders foster "a new internal social architecture . . . that facilitates collaboration among your faculty and staff" (p. 31).

Effective principals establish expectations for students to construct their own learning. Students should own their knowledge, increasing relevance of that knowledge in their present and for their future. Adequate consideration must be given to the efficiency of learning environments seeking to make the entire school day educationally purposeful for the students. Furthermore, a fair and balanced opportunity to learn is essentially important throughout the school.

Data Matters

Exercising an effective approach of using data to inform decision making processes in a statistical and specific manner is an important task of the instructional leader. Schmoker (1999) found that "Data helps us to monitor and assess performance," and "Just as goals are an essential element of success, so data are an essential piece of working toward goals" (p. 35). The focus of data collection, its review, and corresponding decisions should be on reaching the predetermined goals of the school. There is a need for principals to monitor progress toward the goals of the school and make adjustments based on data.

"data are"

Related to school-wide endeavors, data-engaged principals know what goals, initiatives, and processes need to be statistically monitored. Second, principals determine an instrument, timeline, and responsible party for the data collection. Third, principals ensure that monitoring and review takes place in a reliable and valid manner. Fourth, appropriate individuals review the collected data and collaborate for making any necessary adjustments. Finally, after adjustments are made, reflection and process-refinement are important for the school.

Accepting the challenge of being informed by data can be daunting. Williamson and Blackburn (2009) wrote that "Many principals feel as if they are drowning in data, overwhelmed with the sheer amount of data they have, and unsure how to use the information" (p. 20). With the tremendous amount of data accessible for today's principals, chaotic data reviews and sporadic decisions are prevalent. However, when principals keep data relevance focused on specific goal achievement, they have a greater likelihood of successfully achieving those goals for the students.

There is an untrue assumption that weighs on principals regarding the understanding of data. While principals need a lucid understanding of data as it relates to school-wide goals, it is not reasonable for principals to have consumed and internalized data related to every specific student in the school; instead, principals create an expectation that individual classroom teachers utilize data to guide their instruction. Rather than a unit of data storage, principals as servant-leaders consider themselves a resource of effective instruction which utilizes data to improve pedagogical processes.

For the principal, data is viewed as a live report of status or progress. This feedback is meaningful in building individual student growth as well as collective growth. Hattie (1992) concluded that "The most powerful single modification that enhances achievement is feedback" (p. 9). When empirical data is utilized to guide instructional decisions, students benefit from the process. Targeted data usage cannot be neglected by principals seeking school improvement based on increased student learning.

Backward Design

Principals knowledgeable about strategic learning processes understand the value of a backward design of learning. This approach begins with the end results in mind. Many teachers, for various contributing factors, approach learning in the wrong direction and start with instruction. Instead, effective teachers appreciate the expectations of what their students should know and understand as a result of their instruction. Furthermore, these teachers recognize, in advance, what the formative and summative assessments will be.

An effective sequence consists of curricular understanding, assessment planning, instruction, assessment, and teacher reflection and refinement. This process is not so rigid that teacher artistry is denied; instead, teachable moments enhance the process.

As a servant to the learning process, principals benefit from modeling this practice before the faculty. Furthermore, these practices should be firm expectations of the teachers. This approach is highly suggested for schools where accountability corresponds with results of standardized testing.

As an example, successful home-builders have an architectural plan before beginning the project. As they proceed through the stages of construction, they make alterations based on structural concerns or aesthetic creativity. When the house is complete, it should closely resemble the initial plans. However, it should be improved based on technical or artistic augmentation.

The same is true for effective pedagogy as teachers begin with the end result in mind. Thankfully, through the process, teachers paint their nuances of originality and creativity upon the minds of the students. In the end, the minimum educational results are met, along with splashes of lagniappe (a little something extra).

Meaningful Engaged Learning

To provide a quality academic experience, educators must consider the need to capitalize on every moment in contact with their students. With their teacher, students benefit from meaningful engaged learning (MEL). It is highly advantageous for student growth when teachers succeed in their responsibilities of securing positive experiences for all students.

The two primary components of this concept are *meaningful* and *engaged*. One without the other is rendered useless. *Meaningful* ensures processes that are relevant, rigorous, and purposeful while *engaged* requires consistent focus, positive classroom participation, and collaboration between all parties in the learning environment. As an outcome, a meaningfully engaged learner is strategically on-task, internalizing the process, and appreciating their responsibility to their own learning.

To provide an appropriate environment for meaningful engaged learning, teachers must be passionate about the maximizing of instructional connectivity with students. In facilitation of production and positive learning experiences, teachers should utilize multidisciplinary tasks, interactive approaches, collaboration, and student exploration in an authentic sense. Teachers must be acutely aware of when students are meaningfully engaged in their instruction and seek to ensure this level of consistency for the entire learning session.

The expectation for meaningful engaged learning is a trademark of a principal serving the needs of the students. To promote this, principals model effective instruction, team-teach with faculty, frequent classrooms for observation, and provide constant feedback for teachers on their performance in this area. Furthermore, principals should consider student outputs, and not teacher inputs, as the top priority of learning.

Instead of traditional approaches of watching teachers, the focus of observations should be on student outputs as a result of teacher inputs. In general, the question for the principal should be: *What meaningful knowledge or skills have the students obtained as a result of their time spent with the teacher?*

learning Targets

If necessary, principals find ways to quantify meaningful engagement through classroom observation of student learning behaviors. By providing awareness for teachers, instructional practices improve and student learning grows. The greatest possibilities for student and school success, more than any other factor, depend on the quality and impact of classroom instruction. Responsible learning hinges on the principal's willingness and ability to lead effective instructional programing on behalf of the students.

Professional Development

Every year, schools spend large amounts of both time and money on professional development. Unfortunately, seldom does that professional development make sense in terms of those indicators. There is a more efficient and effective manner than existing common practices. The most successful implementation of professional development for the instructional staff is based on reaching the school's vision package.

The development sessions, specifically, are based on assisting the school in meeting the established mission and goals. All professional development should be based on this premise. Whitaker (2003) found that "Outstanding principals know that their primary role is to teach the teachers," and "The best way to provide an exceptional learning environment for students is to give them outstanding teachers" (p 35). As an instructional leader, the effective principal recognizes the need to "teach the teachers" by establishing effective professional development practices to increase teacher knowledge and skills.

PLC's

Professional development, through learning communities, should not be seen as separate events from everyday activity. Instead, it is embedded into the daily learning community of the school through collaborative opportunities. Constant and meaningful professional learning for the instructional staff requires a shifting paradigm for many educators. It is often baffling that the profession that exists to foster learning refuses to embrace similar endeavors for the adults in the building. Barth (2001) noted, "Probably the most important—and the most difficult—job of the school based reformer is to change the prevailing culture of a school" (p. 7).

Consideration should be given as to how the school's master schedule impacts learning. Is the schedule built to accommodate lunch and recess, or is it designed with uninterrupted learning blocks as the primary consideration? The principal arranges the school schedule, allowing for common planning among grade levels or subject areas. Then, during this time, the principal facilitates practices to improve the overall effectiveness of the instructional staff. These professional development sessions are scheduled and systemically planned, but the responsibilities for specific delivery of content may be shared among the administration and teachers.

 Another simple, yet highly effective, method of professional development is peer observation. While principals must be cautious to avoid putting certain teachers on pedestals to avoid risks of alienating morale, it is still quite effective for teachers to learn from observation of their peers. It may take time for this approach to become accepted by all; however, the benefits are tremendous when results are used for collaboration and discussion to improve learning throughout the school. If embarking on this idea, principals should use caution and calculate all possible scenarios of concern.

One key to improved teacher effectiveness is quality, job-embedded professional learning sessions. This should be a collaborative and frequent effort between relevant administrators, teachers, and support staff. Recognizing this opportunity for success, an effective principal utilizes this avenue as a pathway toward reaching the school's vision package.

Literacy Leadership

One of the most fundamental skills necessary for lifetime success is literacy. Therefore, with this in mind, it becomes both a moral and educational imperative to ensure literacy for all students under the principal's umbrella of responsibility. Recently, caring and passionate principals throughout the United States have become intrigued by, or interested in, the idea of literacy leadership as a vehicle for whole-school improvement and, from a humanistic standpoint, see it as a moral obligation to fulfill. Enlightened school leaders realize the dream of democracy requires a literate citizenry and recognize that to a degree, the principal shoulders this duty.

Multiple definitions exist for defining the term *literacy*; however, we will consider *literacy* as the ability to read and write. The importance of individuals gaining literacy is significant because illiteracy substantially and negatively impacts one's life and places long-term burdens on society.

↳ use for goal/mission?

More than any other source, schools must accept the responsibility for ensuring literacy for all students, allowing them to ultimately become functioning members of our democratic society and allowing our democratic quest to continue. As evidenced through a growing body of academic research and empirical data, successful school literacy efforts are vital to lifetime success and require capable and concerned leaders who are tirelessly committed to literacy education from both a technical and programmatic perspective (Carbo 1997).

Principals seeking positive change in the literacy achievement of their students find value in the creation of a literacy-rich culture within the school. Establishing such a culture requires a highly calculated, methodical, and overt approach by an ambitious principal. This culture must be inclusive of effective instruction, vibrant classroom libraries, a well-stocked and inviting school library, literacy competitions, literacy remediation, literacy intervention, interdisciplinary approaches to literacy, and literacy modeling by the adults. All pieces of the literacy puzzle must situate within each other and not be disconnected and futile.

Booth and Rowsell (2007) believe that "Literacy stands as one of the most effective vehicles for school change" because "Literacy ensures the success in other curriculum areas" (p. 21). Principals willing to make a significant commitment to school-wide literacy spend valuable time in such professional-learning activities as literacy-needs determinations, visits to successful literacy campuses, attendance at reputable literacy conferences, and reviews of literacy-related text.

After literacy plans are set forth, principals ensure that teachers have a firm understanding of both the delivery of technical craft and the understanding of programmatic initiatives to support learning in the areas of phonemic awareness, phonics, fluency, vocabulary, and comprehension.

Instructionally, principals set the expectation of effective whole-class instruction (green zone), secondary support remediation for students in need (yellow zone), and intense intervention for the most challenging students (red zone). The efforts to create literacy within every child depend on the principal's ability to motivate and provide the teachers with the necessary resources for diagnosing specific deficits and shoring those deficits with specific responses.

These responsibilities are demanding in the area of literacy leadership; however, without consideration of the grade-level, literacy leadership is important. Every teacher might not be responsible for English or reading instruction, but each teacher should be a literacy teacher in their content area. Teaching content-area vocabulary, for example, is vital. Principals hold the key role for individual students and the entire school to be successful readers and writers.

With success comes excitement and gratification from using the principalship for the common good of literacy for all. Furthermore, through successful literacy leadership, students will find heightened levels of knowledge and understanding, supporting their own knowledge base and the democratic needs of a literate citizenry.

Numeracy Leadership

Although the importance of effectively leading instructional programming in every content area is important, literacy is fundamental and must be understood above all other disciplines. It is the language for understanding other humanistic, historical, and social concepts. Next, and standing alongside literacy, is numeracy. Serving as the language of engineering, science, and many vocational studies, numeracy is the ability to effectively compute and logistically solve mathematical problems.

Unfortunately, as students progress through their school grades, many become exhausted and disgusted with their math classes, leading to struggles in other content areas requiring computation and logic. By the time many students reach high school, they have developed a disdain for numeracy that is difficult to overturn. It is the responsibility of the principal to ensure holistic school practices for numeracy in the same manner as literacy.

To meet the needs of today's students, principals set expectations through discussions, modeling, and faculty professional development addressing best practices in numeracy. Again, effective whole-class instruction should be augmented with remediation, tiered intervention models, interdisciplinary connections with other subjects (such as science), and school-wide endeavors.

Zemelman, Daniels, and Hyde (1998) found that "Because new approaches to mathematics curriculum and teaching in many ways run contrary to conventional wisdom and popular beliefs in our society, the principal should be in the forefront actively promoting best practice in mathematics" (p. 97). In order to accomplish this, principals will need to remain current on research findings for best practices and share these findings through the use of the school's established professional learning community.

If there is not an energetic and noticeable push of numeracy on the campus, it will remain mundane to the students and faculty. The numeracy presence must be significant and overt. Through this, school improvement will take place with the enhancement of individual students in numeracy and throughout other subjects. Furthermore, it will prepare students for lives that will require varying degrees of computation and logic.

Protecting Instructional Time

With the many activities on campus and the involvement of multiple individuals, interruptions to instructional time can become quite frequent. Some examples of this include an intercom break to announce a change in soccer practice, having students out of class for pictures, or allowing students to run errands throughout the school, including selling things or distributing papers.

It is an imperative of the principal, once committed to an effective instructional day, to protect that day at all costs. Without fail, this will lead to challenges from others who do not fully appreciate the value of protected instructional time. Once it is set as a priority, and voiced from the beginning of the year, faculty and students are more accepting of the idea.

There are numerous ways for principals to ensure communication throughout the school without random breaks for announcements. But, once a system is established, fidelity to the system must be ensured. Even brief interruptions of instructional time lead to an idea that it is acceptable to interrupt from time to time. The message should be clear: instructional time is protected from announcements for everything short of emergency situations.

The same philosophy may be adopted for having students out of the classroom for various events. The principal's policy should be clear that students are not to be out of the instructional environment. To accomplish this, the principal is required to be creative in determining how school-wide out-of-class events, such as a pep rallies or picture days, will be handled. Some schools have extended class periods by banking minutes. Then, they use those minutes when needed.

Some schools have created blocks of time during the day for noninstructional activities and, when not needed, these blocks are utilized for enrichment, intervention, or remediation. The methods of scheduling will vary based on the nuances of each individual school; however, if principals voice the expectation that instruction will be protected, it becomes a responsibility of the principal and the talented educators on his or her campus to determine mechanisms to fulfill the protection.

It is unquestionable that even small breaks in student focus decrease learning's maximum potential. Recognizing this, and as a servant to effective instruction, the principal vows to protect the instructional time of faculty and students by taking a stand and following through on the commitment.

Importance of Teacher Observations and Evaluations

One of the most difficult tasks of many principals is the completion of teacher observations and evaluations. Despite the complexity or difficulty of the task, teacher observation and evaluation requires accuracy. This, in most systems, is a measure by which ineffective teachers are recognized for removal, teaching skills are honed, and/or teachers are congratulated and commended for their efforts. Removing those teachers who are criminal in their negligence of proper instruction and the applauding of effective instructors is a way to set high academic expectations and boost morale.

A foremost problem is the lack of a true picture of each teacher. When teachers are informed about an upcoming observation, all but the most inept individuals can put on a *dog-and-pony show*, or façade, for the principal. A key to overcoming this barrier is to increase the intensity of lesson planning, spend more time in classrooms, and invest more time in conversation with teachers. By doing these three things, principals have a better and more reliable sense of what teachers are doing instructionally.

In both observations and evaluations, principals should support all findings with information. If a teacher, for example, receives low marks for using data to support student learning, the principal should also cite supporting examples. The same is true for teachers receiving high marks. Furthermore, teachers in categories of unacceptable overall ratings should receive a remediation plan for improvement.

The ultimate goal of an intensive assistance plan is to support the teacher toward meeting expected standards. This plan also serves as justification if it becomes evident that the teacher is not improving and removal procedures must begin.

Through both observation and evaluation, principals must give teachers constructive feedback and plans for improvement when needed. Additionally, both the principal and the teacher should sign each document and a copy should be provided for both the personnel files and the teacher's personal record. Above all, principals will benefit from strict adherence to the district-accepted policy for teacher observation and evaluation.

FIVE

Organizational Leadership

It's common to say that trees come from seeds. But how could a tiny seed create a huge tree? Seeds do not contain the resources needed to grow a tree. These must come from the medium or environment within which the tree grows. But the seed does provide something that is crucial: a place where the whole of the tree starts to form. As resources such as water and nutrients are drawn in, the seed organizes the process that generates growth. In a sense, the seed is a gateway through which the future possibility of the living tree emerges. —Peter Senge

REFINEMENT OF A LEADER; EVOLUTION OF A SCHOOL

When she walks the tiled hallways, her heels make a pronounced, repetitive clicking and clacking sound on the flooring. Her black business suit and tailored figure sends a message of professional confidence. In conversation, the passion of her tone and specificity of her vocabulary leave little doubt of her ability and willingness to make hard decisions and have fierce conversations. However, despite the aura of her sophisticated being, an investigation of her philosophy and actions represent that of a servant to her school.

As the principal of Parkway High School in Bossier City, Louisiana, Dr. Nichole Bourgeois is a committed steward of a school that provides educational opportunity to a diverse grouping of students. An alumna of PHS, she served as the school's assistant principal in the five years prior to assuming the principalship.

"Several years ago, I was originally hired as the school's assistant principal with areas of focus in curriculum and instruction," Bourgeois said. "However, with the promotion of the assistant principal of administration to another position in the district, I was quickly assigned his former responsibilities and tasked with managing the campus outside of curriculum and instruction."

For Bourgeois, the opportunity to step outside her comfort level of curriculum and instruction proved enormously beneficial in her refinement as a school leader. Through her experiences, her confidence in school management was bolstered, and her abilities were appropriately honed. Through this process, she grew as a professional educator and was groomed to accept the responsibility of the full principalship.

"Being moved from the position of assistant principal of curriculum and instruction to becoming the assistant principal of school administration was a bittersweet moment for me," she said. "What initially seemed uncertain morphed into a valuable experience in my life as I was forced to encounter problems and seek solutions in areas beyond my prior scope of knowledge."

While change is naturally unsettling and often uncomfortable, it is necessary for heightened levels of success. Instead of cynically performing her new duties, she embraced the opportunity for growth that, over time, shaped her views on organizational leadership in a more global perspective.

As her paradigm of thought, Bourgeois believes "Leadership practices cannot exist without comprehensive, effective, and efficient management practices," and continued "The school principal is ultimately responsible and accountable for the management of all aspects of the organization, to ensure effective and efficient operations, delegation of the responsibilities, and utilization of available resources."

Essentially, Bourgeois believes the school must be operationally sound for learning purposes to be maximized. During her time at Parkway, the school has maintained an accountability rating well above the state average. As a new principal, she accepts the responsibility of continued school improvement as she recognizes the impact a twenty-first-century education will have on her students and the future of our society. As a judicious educational leader, she appreciates that she cannot achieve the vision alone as she builds leadership capacity in others to achieve collective goals through streamlined school operations.

"The level of achievement we seek is excellence in our academic programs, excellence in our athletic programs, excellence in our ability to provide a safe and civil environment, excellence in our efforts to serve the school and community, and excellence in our character," Bourgeois said. She continued by passionately communicating that "Every person associated with Parkway will be positively affected by this vision for excellence and I challenge all to embrace this opportunity to be a part of something bigger than ourselves and to be an active participant in becoming what we are meant to become."

With an attitude of commitment over compliance, Bourgeois has embarked on creating integrated organizational practices that create synergistic balance and harmony between various areas of schooling. Impacted by her efforts are organizational components, such as finance, personnel, safety, and school culture. Through planning based on vision, proactive efforts at Parkway have led to numerous positive outcomes. Furthermore, Bourgeois has designed the school to evolve and grow as a learning system.

"We seek to become a smooth operation for the sake of various forms of stakeholder learning," and "Change presents a powerful sense of opportunity." Today, Parkway High School is a model of organizational effectiveness and efficiency. Although structures are not optimal, a cohesiveness of operations is present with an expectation of further positive evolution as a body of stakeholders seeking a prescribed vision.

In a school where expectations are high, Bourgeois is rising to the challenge of leading a school in a continuous process of organizational improvement. Her laborious work is daunting, but she understands her calling to the work. With a clear picture of Parkway's present operations and a desire to constantly sow new seeds of significance, Bourgeois provides herself as a dynamic source of human capital for a cause worthy of her mission.

STANDARD #3

An education leader promotes the success of every student by ensuring management of the organization, operation, and resources for a safe, efficient, and effective learning environment.

HEALTHY ORGANIZATION

An organization, such as a school, must be *healthy* to accomplish its goals and provide positive experiences for its stakeholders. Although the term *healthy* might seem ambiguous, it actually defines the total of an organization operating in both an effective and efficient method. Healthy organizations function, both daily and long term, with procedures and practices that enable the unit to thrive for the benefit of all stakeholders.

Becoming or maintaining a school of gainful evolvement is a responsibility of the principal. In this instance, principals become servants to the organization by designing and implementing an architectural framework for success. The educative and social fabric of the school seeks to find new mechanisms for meaningful gains, reproduces positive elements, and removes inappropriate attitudes or practices.

Taylor, Martin, Hutchinson, and Jinks (2007) found "This search for more effective organizational leadership is an ongoing challenge for any progressive organization or school system dedicated to success," and the "task becomes increasingly important when these organizations are held accountable for demonstrating that success" (p. 402). The current era of accountability requires clear operational management and focused visionary leadership to achieve a healthy school organization.

While the complexities are considerable, the benefits from a healthy school are immense. A primary responsibility of the principal in creating and managing organizational structure is the continued reliance on the school's vision. Furthermore, it is the obligation of the principal to lead the school beyond mediocrity and toward the greatness all stakeholders deserve.

Collins (2001) writes "Good is the enemy of great" and "We don't have great schools, principally because we have good schools" (p. 1). Principals cannot settle for *good*; instead, as servants to the cause, principals are absolutely required, morally and professionally, to have high-functioning, healthy organizations committed to greatness.

The School's Steward

An appropriate descriptor of a principal as servant-leader is *stewardship*. As the leader of the school, the principal is a steward of all stakeholders in the quest to achieve the vision for the school. Bolman and Deal (2001) found that "Successful leaders embody their group's most important values and beliefs" (p. 102). It is necessary, as the organizational steward, to become saturated with the organizational purpose and create collaborative systems for organizational significance and success.

One can visualize the principal, as the steward, guarding the school from any factors of negative influence. Standing with perceptive vigilance, the principal utilizes honor and commitment as the organization's caretaker. Serving as the organizational steward, the principal is a warrior of protection. Just as a loving mother protects her children, a school principal safeguards the school.

A common misconception of servant-leadership renders the leader to a laissez-faire, passive, soft, whimsical, or generally wimpy type of attitude and action. This, of course, is far from reality. Instead, the servant-leader is quite firm in managing school operations and expectations; the servant-leader is not a *pushover*. Drury (2005) noted, "Servant-leadership is a relatively new term for most people, and is often confused with only acts of service, or leadership that only serves, when in fact, this leadership style is more" (p. 10).

As an organizational steward, the principal as servant-leader is very assertive in ensuring organizational health and movement toward the school's vision. The principal will not allow obstacles to become insurmountable and will eliminate nonproductive resistance and actions.

The servant-leader expects high levels of performance, positive attitudes, and mutual respect. Hunter (2004) believed that once expectations

have been established, "It becomes time to turn the organizational structure upside down and help people win" and "The leadership now becomes responsive to those being led by identifying and meeting their
legitimate needs so they can become the best they are capable of becoming and effectively accomplish the stated mission" (p. 51). Servant-leaders are comfortable in their shell and confident in their positional authority; however, they view themselves as a tool to advance the school to its
vision and have solid organizational health.

Barrier Walls

In the late 1980s, there were hopes and signs of the Cold War ending
between the United States and the Soviet Union. There was a strong
American sense that democratic practices would trump the communist
ideas of the Soviets.

The Soviets were enduring serious problems leading to alienation and
suffering of the citizenry. At this same time, a physical and symbolic
Berlin Wall separated a free West Berlin from the Soviet-controlled East
Germany. In the opinion of American President Ronald Reagan, the lack
of individual freedom for the people of East Germany was socially unjust
and morally unacceptable. He viewed freedom as the catalyst for their
progression and equated the communist practices as stifling mechanisms
of control.

During a speech that could be heard on both sides of the Wall, president Reagan essentially declared freedom the victor of the Cold War and
strongly encouraged Mikhail Gorbachev, the Soviet leader, to *tear down
this wall*. A few years later, the wall was tumbled and greater freedoms
were granted to the formerly oppressed.

This story extends beyond a historical reminder. It provides a real
example that when barriers are dismantled, prosperity is constructed.
These lessons are important for the principal seeking a healthy school.
Through reflective practices, principals consider school practices and policies to determine their worth. Additionally, the principal creates safe
opportunities for the faculty, students, and external community to provide feedback for consideration. The perception of a barrier equates to an
actual barrier. Principals willing to make themselves, and their practices,
vulnerable for the sake of improvement are true servants to the school.

The most common barriers preventing optimal organizational health
include activities disconnected from the school's vision, low expectations,
poor communicative practices, and rigid hierarchical structures. On the
contrary, schools with focused programming, high expectations for all,
effective two-way communication, and collaborative teaming across positional lines create positive outcomes.

Removal of barrier walls brings many other benefits, such as increased creativity, improved morale, and beneficial collaboration. When

walls are removed, power is distributed throughout the school and personal accountability becomes the norm for individuals obligated to the school's success. Wheatley (1999) wrote, "The potent force that shapes behavior in these organizations and in all natural systems is the combination of simply expressed expectations of purpose, intent, and values and the freedom for responsible individuals to make sense of these in their own way" (p. 129). Essentially, dismantling barrier walls serves to empower the employees to greater effort and positive results.

Many people believe principals *run the school*. The principal attempting to run the school independently will experience sudden burnout and minimal organizational effectiveness. A judicious principal, to the contrary, understands the value of service through leadership that empowers others to increase the school's overall capacity to achieve. The modern-day father of servant-leadership, Robert Greenleaf (1977), found "The first order of business is to build a group of people who, under the influence of the institution, grow taller and become healthier, stronger, more autonomous" (p. 40).

The term *empowerment* can have negative connotations if suggested in oppressive terms. For example, a principal stating to the school's faculty, *I want to empower you*, could rightfully and easily be considered oppressive. In this context, it presents an unfortunate dichotomy of an owner and the owned. In this sense, the teachers are considered powerless until given power by the principal.

The appropriate approach is one in which the leader models servant-like practices, prompting teachers to take increased levels of ownership and responsibility. Empowering others is more successful when action supersedes words. When barrier walls are removed, the organization flourishes through the capacity of the people.

Matters of Aesthetics

Whether embedded inside an effectively managed organization or looking inward from the outside, there is a striking beauty to the choreography, collegiality, efficiency, methods, and overall orchestration of a purposeful unit of operation. This organizational aesthetic is one that, through seamless operational practices, advances the vision of the school. These progressive steps are liberating for all stakeholders, including the most important individuals on the campus—the students.

There are schools throughout America where organizational havoc and utter chaos prevent the manifestation of quality outcomes for stakeholders. Similarly, there are schools where inconsistency and an unconscious lack of refined focus create markedly inappropriate settings for individuals to live democratically and continually evolve in a purposeful manner. To create an aesthetic school, principals realize the personal dimension of the organization for the stakeholders. With this understanding, principals ensure organizational management that promotes a structure conducive to success and reduces obstacles that stymie smooth transactions of growth.

In consideration of effective leadership, Murphy and Beck (1994) found that "Schools exist for and because of persons and assuming, therefore, that organizational and personal good are not inherently contradictory, these leaders see service of schools and their inhabitants as foundational to their work" (p. 9). In essence, effective school leaders create organizational structure for the individual good of the stakeholders, leading to a collective and beautiful greatness.

To further understand a polished organizational aesthetic, consider the workings of a fine and charming grandfather clock. The transparent workings of the machine are seductively rhythmical and constant. Every component continually performs its requirements and is accountable to the clock as a whole. Without the continued effort of one instrument, time will literally stand still, and the clock no longer serves its purpose. However, when all parts are functioning, an aesthetically beautiful process and product is rendered. Much like this grandfather clock, schools must be connected, continuous, purposeful, and transparent to induce organizational achievement.

A Safe Place

Schools exist for the purpose of systematically facilitating educative experiences for students. However, and possibly surprising to many, student learning is not the primary responsibility of the principal. The most crucial responsibility is to ensure the safety of the students and employees under the dutiful care of the principal.

Each day, across America, approximately one hundred million students leave their parents' arms for the schoolhouse. These parents rightfully expect their children to return safely home from school each afternoon. There must be an unwavering understanding of every principal that student safety is the top responsibility for every school day.

In leading a calculated effort to create a safe place for students, the principal creates and leads a crisis-management team. The responsibilities of this committee include crisis management for the most terrible of events, such as inclement weather or even school terrorism.

It is impossible to prepare for every specific risk to student safety; however, it is important to keep safety a priority focus in the minds of all campus stakeholders. Williamson and Blackburn (2009) wrote that school safety is a responsibility in which principals "invest tremendous energy and time in covering every contingency" while hoping the plan is never required for implementation (p. 165).

There are a number of nonterroristic threats to schools on a daily basis. Most of these threats are weather-related; however, examples of accidental problems include chemical or gas exposure, train derailments, and facility structural instability. Consideration is given to all possible accidental encounters the school could experience.

The crisis-management team may conduct a focused walk through the interior and exterior of the school, along with a drive through the community to highlight these specific areas of concern. Once potential threats have been identified, the crisis-management team develops plans for protecting lives in the event of these disasters. Next, they must be communicated to appropriate individuals as needed.

A second and increasing threat to our schools and students comes from terrorism. The most common form of school terrorism comes from within the school. Typically, these are male students who believe they have experienced rejection or mistreatment from others. The names of these students do not deserve mention; however, principals questing to maintain a safe place for students learn from these deadly experiences.

Relationships are tremendously important in avoiding terroristic events on school campuses. In most documented cases, someone on the campus knew the student's plans for terror before it transpired. Had those students felt comfortable in sharing this knowledge with some adult on the campus, through a developed relationship, these events could possibly have been prevented and lives saved. Research tells us that student–mentor relationships, either structured or by chance, are positive forces and lead to increased student-to-school communication. As a proactive principal, constant communication and modeling should support the importance of open relationships on campus.

open relation-ships to help foster exchange of info from students to school

The crisis-management team pays careful attention to both prevention and in-crisis actions. The team enlists the cooperation of local fire control, law enforcement, and medical service organizations when determining possible threats, minimizing the chances of threat, and managing terrorism if it were to happen. Detailed plans that clearly articulate the who, what, when, where, and why should be developed and communicated to the appropriate adults within the building. Furthermore, these drills should be practiced by the school's employees, along with the fire department, law agencies, and medical services.

Careful consideration is given to keep crisis-management plans in the hands of the adults and not students. Furthermore, adults take responsibility for the safety of the students through practice drills as students are not included in specific drills of terrorist crisis management. The purpose for not allowing student involvement is to prevent critical information from getting into the possession of potential student-terrorists.

President Dwight Eisenhower was correct in noting that "Plans are nothing; planning is everything." As servants to families and students, principals frequently plan and prepare for the unforeseen and unimaginable. While the actual plan may prove useless in a time of crisis, individuals will draw from their experiences with the planning process, including their practice, which may save the lives of students in a threatening situation.

In the case of crisis management, *failure to plan* is most definitely *planning to fail*. The primary responsibility of the school principal is the safety of those students under the school's care. Moreover, this reality can never escape the mind of the principal and is always at the forefront.

Utilizing Change

Change in society is a constant force. Schools, as microcosms of our society, are impacted by these changes or societal shifts. Principals cannot avoid outside-forced change, either from society at large or educational policy, from impacting the practices and procedures within their schools. Clever leaders, however, identify ways to utilize change that seeks to benefit the vision package and stays focused on the school's values and mission.

Jenlink (2004) wrote, "Whereas education gravitates to the center of society, education becomes a response to society's tensions and issues as well as a medium for society's hope of an alternative future" (p. 227). In essence, school leaders determine how the organization may benefit from the prescribed changes and utilize the change for the good of the school.

Change is perceived as a problem for many school leaders, causing them to feel a need for compliance as opposed to commitment. And, with the bureaucracy that surrounds the educational system, it is easy to understand this manner of thinking. Unfortunately, this paradigm of thought does not lead to productive gains for the organization or the stakeholders depending on its success. In consideration of change, many believe the best approach is to *manage* change.

The idea of *managing* change is not effective, however, because it implies a reactionary approach. The conscientious servant-leader employs intelligence, foresight, and teaming to anticipate and cultivate change for the betterment of the organization. Duffy (2003) believes that changes initiated from outside the walls of the school "is nonlinear and requires educators to seek controlled disequilibrium that provides the energy needed to create innovative opportunities for improvement" (p. 65). Effective principals enlist the capacity of their team and determine school-specific ways to usher in change and benefit the whole.

A different form of change is school-imposed change. School-imposed change is the common practice of identifying a need and making a change in school policy or practice to help move the school toward its vision package. In order to operate more effectively and efficiently, school principals make changes each day of their employment.

Change is a necessary force in our schools; if schools remain frozen in current practices, they stagnate or decay. Conversely, schools recognizing the need for continued improvement make needed changes to advance the organization—which leads to a dynamic setting for leading, learning, and working. Ushering change into a school is seldom an easy undertaking for the principal, especially changes that disrupt current school culture. Hunter (2004) found that "Changing years of ingrained habits and behaviors requires a great deal of commitment and effort" and "Many people are simply not up to the task" (p. 164).

Principals as servant-leaders to their schools readily change, or shift, ineffective school cultures by pruning inappropriate personalities, practices, and programs. Principals do not stand by and allow anything to hinder the school from effective and efficient organizational flow. When initiating change, principals must utilize teaming when possible, communicate rationale, clarify processes, implement wisely, reflect on value, and refine as needed. As caring and passionate educators, principals utilize their positional authority to create opportunities for both the organization and its members to flourish.

Conscientious principals benefit from a greater understanding of systemic change theory. The purpose of briefly illuminating change in this discourse, however, is not to provide a theory or toolkit. Fullan (2008) suggested that individual leaders define their own change theories because if they "look for silver bullets and techniques, there is too much to remember, and you will not understand them deeply enough to use them" (p. 125).

The hope is for principals to appreciate the need for anticipating and responding to outside change and to actively initiate school-imposed change for the benefit of the organization when necessary. Above all, principals must utilize change for the betterment of the organizational unit as it seeks to achieve its predetermined vision.

Communication

Within every school, there is communication between stakeholders. The responsibility of the principal, as a servant to the organization, is to ensure that school communication remains focused, open, and positive. Within a school, there are many forms of communication, including effective messaging to and from the principal.

Well-intentioned principals throughout America fail to lead a successful school because of communication deficits. Some common examples include poor speaking and writing skills, faulty approaches to communication that leave others disgusted, and a lack of value for the importance of communication. This skill of communication, although studied minimally in most preparation programs, has an underestimated power and is often taken for granted by principals. By challenging the school to find ways to inform itself, through open and purposeful communication, principals find significant organizational benefits.

All communication is relational to other people. The overall impression gained by an audience typically comes from 55 percent nonverbal expression of the speaker, 38 percent from the vocal quality of the speaker, and 7 percent of what the speaker actually says (Mehrabian 1981). It is important to remember that 93 percent of someone's impression has little to do with the actual message. This ratio is true for both private conversations and group addresses.

Principals would benefit from honing their ability to relate to others via appropriate nonverbal communication, word articulation, and voice projection, depending on the context. A simple suggestion is to ask others for constructive feedback in these areas.

The vision, mission, and goals of the school must be the driving forces for all communicative practices. No matter the reason, setting, or required conversation/speech/memo, the principal as servant to the organization must situate the dialogue in terms of the school's vision.

One helpful idea is to consider how spoken or written words will advance people toward the overarching vision or goals. This approach is not naïve or simplistic; in fact, it takes a skilled communicator to achieve this result. Another reason to align communication toward the vision is unintended or multiple interpretations of a message. If communication remains focused on ways to reach the vision, the interpretations should be more targeted and the initial intent more clearly understood.

Effective communication reduces the amount of reactive behaviors from principals. Regarding information that needs to be spread (not confidential), it is important to get the message out in advance. When individuals know of certain events, needs, or initiatives in advance, they have ample time to ask questions, gain clarity, plan, and anticipate.

When information is not provided in advance, this leads to confusion, poor implementation, and lower morale. Frontloading reduces the need to be reactive at later times and is a proactive measure for organizational health. It is much better for stakeholders to hear the focused message from the principal in advance, than from faculty workroom gossip or community rumblings.

An *open-door* policy means more than an open door. One of the most common phrases used by principals is *I have an open-door policy*. However, having an open door only allows access to the principal. While access is foundational, stakeholders must feel comfortable sharing ideas, voicing concerns, and problem solving while in the principal's office.

Understanding the value of relationships, the principal must believe office visitors are the most important people in the world during the time of that encounter. By doing this, that visitor will sense their value and relationships will be forged. Even when outcomes are not agreeable to both parties, it is important for all stakeholders to feel valued.

Instead of talking *to* people, principals as servant-leaders talk *with* people. If in the office, principals should move from around their desk to sit with their visitor. This simple task removes the sense of dictatorial presence the principal might otherwise create. If out of the office, try to mirror the person's actions.

Psychology indicates that by creating our body positioning similar to that of others, we are more accepted by the other person. For example, if the stakeholder crosses arms, the principal should subtly do the same. This might sound silly; however, various studies indicate that simple body mirroring enhances nonverbal communication's benefit. Next, the principal actively listens to others and asks clarifying questions as needed to gain a better sense of understanding.

When the person has finished speaking, the principal may recite the main points back to the person to check for understanding. From this point, a shared understanding, solution, or exchange of knowledge should take place. At the end of each conversation, there should be clarity on what the next steps are and the responsible parties.

Effective communication is vital to success. Principals serve their schools well by studying processes of communication, understanding the specific needs of stakeholders, and self-reflecting on communicative practices. Furthermore, principals must remember to take a back seat to the people and purpose of the school. If the communicator becomes larger than the messages communicated, a problem exists. A sense of humility must be present in all conversations, speeches, and written communication.

School-Based Financial Decisions

Providing a free, appropriate public education for the elementary and secondary students within the United States requires tremendous amounts of federal, state, and local funding. While figures vary, it is estimated by the U.S. Department of Education that combined spending from all three governmental levels exceeds six hundred billion dollars annually.

Based on levels from the Reagan administration of the 1980s, spending has exponentially outpaced inflationary rates and has basically increased by nearly 150 percent during the past fifteen years. Unfortunately, during this same time frame, overall academic achievement and graduation rates have been marginal at best.

As stewards of the organization's public funds, school leaders must ensure a significant return on investment through sound educational endeavors that mirror a commitment to fiscally responsible monetary practices. While processes for allocation differ throughout the nation, the site-based principal accepts a reasonable degree of accountability and responsibility once public funds are channeled to the campus. The degree to which principals have monetary control depends upon systems in place by the superintendent and the district's business department.

As passionate educators, effective principals view funds under their control as fuel for the school's educational vehicle. While money is *expended* in advancing the school and its students toward the predetermined vision, mission, and goals, it is an *investment* into the futures of individual students and the society of the future. Furthermore, it is incredulous to believe that American taxpayers deserve school principals who frivolously and erroneously waste funds dedicated to student learning and the continuation of democratic ideals.

While societal ills are an understood extraneous variable to collective deficits in academic achievement growth, committed principals find this excuse unacceptable and quest to overcome all adversity and challenges to student learning. Sensibly, an increase in funds should correspond with an increase in achievement. A primary problem, however, is the often capricious and nonpurposeful utilization of available funds by school principals. While no principal has infinite funds, it is the responsibility of the principal to conscientiously align accessible funds with specific goals.

In consideration of spending, rational principals utilize the approach of goal-based budgeting. This method recalls the overarching purpose for the organization, along with the specific goals for the school year, and allocates the fiscal year budget to advance the school toward those needs.

Smith and Lynch (2004) define *budget* as a "plan for the accomplishment of programs related to objectives and goals within a definite time period, including an estimate of resources required, together with an estimate of the resources available, usually compared with one or more past periods and showing future requirements" (p. 38). This operational definition is perfect consideration for principals to understand the importance of matching funds to a purpose. When principals perform this technique and maintain organizational clarity, the school has a greater propensity for reaching its goals.

With an appreciation of educational funds as an investment and goal-based budgeting, it is also meaningful and advantageous for principals to accurately manage their processes through appropriate accounting protocol. Brimley and Garfield (2001) assert that "There is little to question or to criticize when there are accurate and verified financial records of a school's operations" while "On the other hand, shoddy or inadequate records can serve to impugn the actions of those in charge, even where there has been no dishonest intent" (p. 319). *Keep good accurate records!*

To guarantee adequate accounting practices, principals remain cognizant of and follow established controls, adhere to the Government Accounting Standards Board (GASB) expectations, and consult with their district business department's documents and personnel as needed.

With forethought, prudence, and accuracy, school principals utilize available funds to meet desired needs. Furthermore, these sound practices lead to increased trust from the American taxpayers and advance the school toward its organizational vision package.

Dangerous Delegating

Wise principals surround themselves with ambitious, competent, and innovative employees. This practice is a successful model for improving organizational health and advancing the school in creative and effective ways. In doing so, principals as servant-leaders release control of various components of organizational operations, allowing the hired talent an opportunity to produce amazing results. In his book on leadership, former New York City mayor Rudy Giuliani (2002) dedicates an entire chapter to surrounding oneself with great people. There is little doubt that strong and talented employees benefit both principal's work and the school's overall effort.

Effective organizational leadership requires an understanding of the responsibilities and expectations of each employee. Although servant-leadership requires extreme sharing of power and collaborative responses, it also demands the facilitation of streamlined organizational processes where everyone involved knows the specific responsibilities for which they will be held accountable.

As the point person for the school, the principal delegates responsibilities and tasks to appropriate talent. There is, however, an unfortunate pitfall of delegating responsibility for principals to avoid.

Often, when tasks are delegated, they are not completed in alignment with the school's vision package. Furthermore, the actions may not be acceptable to the principal, causing reactive responses to the outcome and the employee charged with the initial responsibility. This leads principals to internalize such thoughts as *If I want it done right, I have to do it myself* or *If it's worth doing, it's worth doing yourself.* In order to avoid such comments and have tasks completed to the satisfaction of the principal, it is necessary to initiate progress checks and keep the doors of communication overtly open about the task.

As a servant, the principal provides employees with support and resources necessary to achieve their responsibilities. While employees creatively attend to their duties, the principal maintains contact, providing guidance as needed. It is not acceptable for principals to "hand-off" tasks and never provide support or input for the individual primarily tasked with the responsibility. The accountability for all aspects of schooling belongs to the school principal.

Matters of Student Behavior

Structured schools have a listing of universally accepted and understood behavioral expectations for the student body. These expectations serve to guide the code of conduct for students. Examples of appropriate expectations to be applied and taught to students include respecting others, accepting responsibility, respecting oneself, and respecting property. When students fail to meet these simple expectations, they receive a negative consequence such as loss of privileges. On the contrary, when students routinely meet expectations, they receive a positive consequence such as an extrinsic or intrinsic personalized or class reward.

The conscientious and caring school is proactive in establishing a behavior-consequence plan for students related to daily student encounters and school management. The behavior consequence plan includes all measures for maintaining a safe and appropriate campus and is inclusive of both negative and positive consequences for student behavior. For example, students not meeting an established expectation might receive a negative consequence while students performing as expected would receive, on occasion, positive consequences.

This concept of behavior management reinforces the notion that every individual choice in life creates some form of consequence, either negative or positive. Historically, plans for student control have been in place and are known as the school's discipline plan. It is important to refrain from using this outdated terminology as discipline equates a sense of punishment to students and does not fully explore notions of life's causal consequences relating to personal choice.

Once the behavior-consequence plan is developed, it should be appropriately communicated to students and parents. The communication of the plan's rationale and actions create a sense of trust and eliminate problems later. The plan is utilized by the school's leadership to provide consequences for student actions, such as teacher referrals to the office for a student's poor behavior or a reward structure for a student who repeatedly meets the established expectations.

Teachers within the school need to feel supported by leadership in addressing inappropriate student actions. At the same time, however, principals have an expectation of teachers that all avenues have been exhausted within the classroom setting before students are referred to the office for a negative consequence. Once a student is referred to the office, the principal, or administrative designee, must thoroughly investigate the situation and properly apply consequences, if needed.

It is vitally important that administrators afford students both procedural and substantive due process through the behavior investigation, *due process* hearing, and enforced consequence. Additionally, principals utilize this time with the student for remediation of the behavioral expectations and overall counseling. This is also an opportunity for collaboration with the student's parent or guardian, which may or may not be a positive experience.

Before a student leaves the principal's office, if found guilty of the charges, the principal does everything within ability to ensure the student understands the charges, the expectations, and the consequence.

Furthermore, it is imperative that principals never strip students of their dignity while in such conferences. These principal and student collaborations, even when prompted by inappropriate behavior, serve as opportunities to build relationships and teach expectations.

Principals exert much effort addressing, proactively, but sometimes reactively, inappropriate student behavior. The other side of the coin is providing positive consequences as rewards for students meeting, or exceeding, expectations. Plans will be very unique to every school; however, overt consideration is due in regard to those students who meet expectations. It is a great school culturing opportunity to reward students when they rise to the occasion, make themselves proud, or show marked improvement.

Much argument exists within the educational community regarding the rewarding of student behavior. Critics insist that educators should not reward students for actions they *should be doing anyway*. In contrast, it is important to note that rewards provide teachable opportunities to highlight student achievement or growth in a number of areas including academics, behavior, and social settings.

Rewarding students does not always require extrinsic factors that cost large sums of money; instead, most rewards are actually words of encouragement, praise, or support, which build authentic relationships of trust, mutual understanding, and respect. Students, for all their efforts, deserve to receive an occasional positive consequence for their actions. Through efforts of providing these positive consequences, the importance of all actions having some form of consequences and positive decision making leading to positive results is reinforced.

The overall goal of consequences is to improve student decision making in the future. Many lose sight of this goal and reduce the art of consequence to a barbaric attempt to punish. Insightful principals realize that consequences are a method of teaching and serve as catalysts for the building of positive relationships and student evolvement.

SIX

Collaborative Leadership

We could learn a lot from crayons: some are sharp, some are pretty, some are dull, while others are bright, some have weird names, but we have to learn to live in the same box. — Anonymous

A STORY OF RENEWAL

A.A. Nelson Elementary School in Lake Charles, Louisiana, has become a premier setting for learning. As a collegial team, the administration, faculty, parents, and community share mutual respect and a dynamic passion for student learning. Their student achievement, as determined by standardized testing, draws attention from those seeking a model of effective elementary schooling.

Their success is not a story of reform; instead, it's a narrative of educational renewal. A.A. Nelson Elementary was doing really well; then, they noticed a dip in their performance. Realizing correction was necessary, Principal Jacqueline Smith responded. Instead of sweeping reforms at the already successful site, she renewed the culture of collaboration and focused to improve student achievement. While there was not a single area for transformation, she led gradual changes to bring clarity of purpose back to the school. And, it worked.

Within time, the school's accountability rating regained its former prominence. Then, the school succeeded the former standards of excellence altogether. Over the past four years, A.A. Nelson Elementary has increased school performance scoring by 16 percent. Smith gives credit to a village of committed stakeholders for the success of the school. She believes "Our school has always been based on strong collaboration."

The 2012 Louisiana Elementary Principal of the Year considers her approach as one of shared leadership. Smith said, "I accept input in decision making and problem solving" but, in acceptance of responsibility, she clarified, "I retain the final say when choices are made." The stakeholders seem to value her authenticity and credibility because of her inclusive nature. Proudly, she noted, "People would definitely say that I am a collaborative leader!" Her basis for this quote is formed from believing input leads to better decisions and that effective delegation is important.

Her collaborative methods of working together tap the expertise of many participants. Smith said, "This style tends to lead to more accurate and productive decisions, since I do not claim to be an expert in every area" and "This type of process is motivational and creates an environment based on respect." She recognizes the talents of the faculty through delegation, providing them resources and follow-up. Smith shared, "As a leader, I depend on qualified and trustworthy employees to help attain our goals" and "Teachers enjoy being part of a collaborative team."

The environment of A.A. Nelson Elementary is respectful and inclusive of all. Students enjoy their time at the school and teacher turnover is very low. Smith boldly expressed the school has "a family-like and nurturing environment" and continued by sharing "There is a lot of love at our school and this is the main reason that our students are so successful and our staff is so happy."

The spoken words of the principal are not fictional. An A.A. Nelson Elementary parent stated, "This school has so much to offer beyond the normal drop your kid off at eight and pick them up at three" because "This is more like a small community with many friends, great leaders, and most of all great kids!" With a collaborative culture questing for excellence, on behalf of children, A.A. Nelson Elementary will continue to draw attention as an effective school serving students and their futures.

STANDARD #4

An educational leader promotes the success of every student by collaborating with faculty and community members, responding to diverse community interests and needs, and mobilizing community resources.

TOGETHER EVERYONE ACHIEVES MORE (TEAM)

School leaders work in an environment of individual personalities, cliques, groups, organizations, factions, teams, and other collections of associated persons. The necessity to be all things to all people is a complex, daunting, and required task. Knowing this, it is seemingly impossible for a principal to effectively lead without a basic understanding and implementation in practice of collaborative processes.

Individuals holding superb natural leadership traits cannot achieve sustained school leadership success without the ability to effectively relate, respond, rally, and respect the diverse collection of stakeholders. Leadership is reduced when the troop feels alienated, disconnected, or unwanted.

Within time, a noncollaborative leader's power of influence will fade, resulting in the principal clinging to positional authority *over* people instead of *with* people. In contrast, principals who communicate through their actions the authentic value for people find that Together Everyone Achieves More (TEAM).

The value of an efficient and effective collaborative team is great for the school. The benefits include improved instruction through teaming, increased morale through contentment and worth, and a greater likelihood of reaching the school's vision package. To grow positive capacity within stakeholders requires a collaborative principalship approach based on relationships.

A majority of a principal's daily work is relational, and success depends on the principal's ability to generate initial and strengthen existing relationships. Wheatley (1999) found "The era of the rugged individuals has been replaced by the era of the team player" and "More and more relationships are in store for us, out there in the vast web of life" (p. 39).

As a paradigm shift, the image of a dictatorial principal towering over the school is transformed to a principal working alongside others, facilitating processes that advance the school to collective ends. The evolvement of the role serves as an adaptation to the leadership expectations of today's stakeholders who understand and appreciate their rights to be heard and included in democratic ways.

Foster (1989) believed leadership "is the ability of humans to relate deeply to each other in the search for a more perfect union" and is a "consensual task, a sharing of ideas, and a sharing of responsibilities, where a 'leader' is a leader for the moment only, where the leadership exerted must be validated by the consent of the followers, and where leadership lies in the struggles of a community to find meaning for itself" (p. 61).

A judicious principal recognizes the value and potential of the whole is greater than the value of the individual parts in isolation. Furthermore, the principal capitalizes on potential through teams and networks that proactively approach the needs of the school or, in time, respond to alarms.

Principals as servant-leaders assume servant status to promote individual growth and development, meeting their specific needs. Servant-leaders cheerlead for both employees and students while providing authentically constructive criticism for refinement when necessary. This relational approach is easily detectable when inauthentic. Stone, Russell, and Patterson (2003) believe the servant-leader is "one who focuses on his or her followers" and values the "people who constitute the organization" (p. 5). Without a team, there is no need for a coach. Without students and teachers, there is no need for a principal.

Working with others, in collaboration, has enormous potential in organizations. Spears (2005) found that "traditional, autocratic, and hierarchical modes of leadership" are yielding to "teamwork and community" where leaders "seek to involve others in decision making" (p. 30). Through collaboration, opposing ideas are voiced, collective plans are created, and workload is often reduced. In an educational era when the demands are enormous, successful principals engage everyone's intelligence and abilities for the good of the school.

Serve First

In the Christian faith, a Biblical account clearly articulates the need for servant-leaders. Jesus, the son of God, provides His ordinary disciples with several extraordinary opportunities during their time of training. During one such event, the earthly body of Jesus was transfigured to a heavenly form for three of His closest disciples (Peter, James, and John). The site was so majestic, it caused the disciples to fall to their faces in glory.

Shortly afterward, the disciples were traveling without Jesus along a road and sinfully arguing about who, amongst the group, was the greatest of all. Each disciple, arrogantly and selfishly, declared their own worth as the most valuable. At the conclusion of their trip, the group met back with Jesus, and He questioned them about their conversation. The group, feeling embarrassed and shocked of His knowledge of the conversation, grew silent.

As a teacher, Jesus seized the opportunity to grow the disciples and said, "If anyone desires to be first, he shall be last of all and servant of all" (Mark 9:35). His message clearly communicated His desire for them to be servant-leaders to the Kingdom of God and others throughout the lands.

American psyche has been infiltrated with abnormal views of leaders. Developing an understanding of serving first and leading second requires shifting our mindscapes toward new ways of thinking. McGee-Cooper and Trammell (2002) found "Servant-leadership stands in sharp contrast to the typical American definition of the leader as a stand-alone hero" (p. 143). Instead, the leader provides direction and helps others achieve success for the organization. Success is the only option.

To become a servant-leader, one must counter the *ego-driven power moves* that take the spotlight off the organization and onto the leader's talents, abilities, and accomplishments (Schuster 1998, 272). Instead, Hunter (2004) believes servant-leadership "becomes responsive to those being led by identifying and meeting their legitimate needs so they can become the best they are capable of becoming and effectively accomplishing the stated mission" of the organization (p. 51).

Principals as servant-leaders are energized in their work by helping others fulfill their individual roles as the school moves toward shared goals. Principals as servant-leaders do not require supernatural abilities or talents; instead, they require a humble willingness of continued learning and growth to collaboratively move the school forward through effective practices.

Right Bus, Right Seat

There is a cliché growing in frequency that calls for leaders to get the *right people on the bus*; furthermore, there are calls to get them in the *right seat* once they are on board. Moreover, leaders must *get the wrong people off the bus*.

In relation to the principalship, this means purging the school of ineffective teachers, hiring proper fits for the school, and shuffling existing personnel to match strengths to needs. The school principal, as a servant, could be considered as either the bus driver or the navigator. Achieving the organizational purpose, without the right team, is not likely. Collins (2001) wrote, "Great vision without great people is irrelevant" (p. 42).

First, as discussed in an earlier chapter, there is a requirement to remove ineffective teachers from the campus. There are two situations that might exist. The first includes a quality teacher who is simply a poor fit for a particular campus. The second includes inadequate teacher quality based on such factors as ethics, instruction, management, planning, or professionalism.

No matter the condition, the principal must utilize district procedures to remove or transfer these hindrances from the campus. As a servant to the organization, the principal must take bold stands to promote school success and safeguard the learning environment for children. This requires courageously addressing uncomfortable personnel issues.

Decisions related to human capital vary from district to district, with school-based hiring having more influence in some districts and less in others. If total control of hiring is district based, the principal would benefit from a close relationship with the district human-resources administrator that involves conversations about site-specific needs. If site-based hiring is practiced, principals should utilize strategic measures for finding the right employees for positions.

Consideration should be given to each candidate's offerings for the school. Too often, principals hire based on a specific need and don't consider potential shifts throughout the school to employ the best people with most offerings to the team. It is important to not have a tunnel vision approach to hiring; instead, look at the larger picture of value-added to a campus because of an employment opening. Then, find a way to make all the pieces fit together.

It makes sense to utilize a school-based hiring team to make staffing decisions. Led by the principal, this group interviews each candidate using a prepared rubric for scoring. After each candidate, the group discusses their perceptions of the candidates' ability to effectively fit at the particular school.

The process allows for many positive benefits. One of the positive outcomes includes immediate buy-in, or investment, from key faculty to the selected employee. Wise, Darling-Hammond, and Berry (1987) found that evoking collaborative processes "enhances the validity of the process by providing greater insight into the candidates' subject matter competence" (p. viii). As a side benefit to the leader, if the hire was a mistake, the principal doesn't bear the error alone. Furthermore, this process serves as an indirect marketing event of a school of collaborative and democratic processes.

Once the committee has determined a lead candidate, a second interview with the top choice is facilitated. During the second interview, the principal communicates expectations and a need for loyalty to student achievement and school improvement from the candidate. After a satisfactory second interview, the candidate may be recommended for hire.

Also, principals should consider the utilization of multiple information sources throughout the interview process to include portfolios, having candidates teach sample lessons, writing samples, student data, and calling references. It is vitally important to properly screen a candidate on the front end rather than discovering flaws on the back end. Proactive maneuvering leads to better teacher selections.

Once a new teacher is hired, the work really begins. Principals are then responsible for onboarding the teacher by providing an appropriate induction program for the teacher, assigning a mentor, and providing necessary resources. The goal is to nurture and grow the new teacher through a supporting and collaborative atmosphere of guidance.

The team should be stronger because of their addition to the school. Whitaker (2003) wrote, "Once we hire new teachers it's tempting to wonder how to spread their energy and excitement to the other teachers . . . our first challenge, however, is to keep the new teachers enthusiastic" (p. 43).

Through a process of gradual assimilation, the principal shifts responsibilities to the new teacher and furthers the new teacher's opportunity to provide positive influence on the school as a whole. Through cultivation of every teacher and an increased leadership capacity, the job of the principal only becomes easier with fewer fires to extinguish and fences to mend.

Inspire

During the Texas Revolution in the early 1800s, a group of about two hundred men fortified a mission in San Antonio known as the Alamo. Among these men, including Texan Army and volunteers, were Colonel William Travis (a notorious military officer), Jim Bowie (the famous knife-maker), and Davy Crockett (the legendary American frontiersman). Their hope, in summary, was to resist Mexican advancement into Texas for purposes of Independence.

The general of the Mexican army, Antonio Lopez de Santa Anna, began assembling an army of 6,000 with a goal of pushing into Texas and squelching the revolt of the rebel Texans. The Mexican army arrived much sooner in San Antonio than the Texans anticipated.

With slightly more than 200 men, the Texans in the Alamo were greatly outnumbered by nearly 6,000 Mexican troops surrounding it. Recognizing this adversity, Colonel Travis sent out messengers for troop reinforcement. His requests never became a reality. General Santa Anna offered surrender to the Texans; however, they denied the request and fired a canon in response to the offer, which indicated their intent to remain steadfast.

Legend holds that Colonel Travis gathered the troops before the battle and drew a line in the sand with his sword. He offered every member the opportunity to stay on one side of the line if they wanted to attempt escape. Everyone wanting to stay in defense was asked to step over the line. His words and the cause were inspiring. In their courage, all but one man stepped over the line. With a small, motivated group, the Alamo would make its stand against the Mexican Army.

Although exact numbers are not universally accepted, it is believed that approximately 1,800 Mexican soldiers stormed the Alamo, killing all but a handful of men. Those not killed within the walls of the Alamo were later executed by General Santa Anna. It should be noted, however, that this group of Texans, fighting for the prize of freedom, killed upwards of 600 Mexican soldiers during the Battle of the Alamo.

The victims of the Alamo did not die in vain. About a month later, led by General Sam Houston, the Texas army overwhelmed General Santa Anna and his Mexican army. In their victorious attack, the Texans charged the Mexican camp with shouts of "Remember the Alamo." During this event, General Santa Anna was captured, and a pathway was cleared to secure Texan independence.

Those men killed in the Alamo knew the costs associated with their commitment to remain on the team. However, their willingness to serve the cause formed their purpose and inspiration. There will be times when principals, like Colonel Travis, must draw lines in the sand to clarify purpose and commitment to the team. It can become one of those *with us or against us* moments — they are either on or off the bus.

Inspiration is an intriguing concept to study and deeply understand. At its core, it serves to build or ignite fires within the beings of individuals. It involves finding ways to change the desires of people to influence their future decisions. Hunter (2004) noted that "Motivation is people moved to action because they *want* to act and they *want* to give their best and their all for the team" (p. 187).

Highly effective principals are typically exceptionally inspirational for their teams. First, it is important to place motivation in the correct context. With the right people in the right seats on the bus, there should be little need for extrinsic motivation of employees. However, it is often crucial to motivate with a focus of the specific vision package of the school in mind. Inspiration, in this sense, is a form of laser-focusing on a desired outcome.

The most consistent form of motivation is fair and equitable practices from the school leader. Eade (1996, n.p.) found the easiest way to motivate employees is to "treat them the same way you wish to be treated: as responsible professionals," and if you "strike the right balance of respect, dignity, fairness, incentive, and guidance . . . you will create a motivated, productive, satisfying, and secure work environment."

As leaders work within their organizations, they have expectations of employees. To generate positive morale and effectiveness within the organization, the employees must see a leader worth following. Greenleaf (2001) offers the following critical questions: "Who is this moral individual we would see as leader? Who is the servant? How does one tell a truly giving, enriching servant from the neutral person or the one whose net influence is to take away from or diminish other people?" (p. 56). Without a doubt, modeling is needed for principals to gain credibility, an important trait needed for leadership.

Servant-leadership develops a sense of autonomy and intrinsic satisfaction within individuals to work and succeed; therefore, encouragement and affirmation from an extrinsic source are not as prevalent as in other leadership constructs. Greenleaf (2001) notes that servant-leaders "work in wondrous ways" to get the most out of others (p. 42). Spears (2005) found that servant-leaders have "intrinsic value" and recognizes the need for "encouraging worker involvement" (p. 35).

If servant-leaders perceive a need, whether encouragement or affirmation, they service those needs for the betterment of both the individual and the organization. In short, as Moxley (2002) explains, leaders "motivate and inspire" others for the greater good of the whole (p. 47). If principals lead with fairness, motivation is increased through a balance of humility, intellect, and progress.

Of course, however, there are occasions where inspirational speeches or conversations might be necessary to motivate individuals, groups, or the whole. If this approach is taken, it is important to keep the message focused on the vision package. And, with all respect, the message is more important than the messenger. There is no *I* in *team*. As servant to the school, when motivation is needed, the principal must motivate. Organizational health depends on the principal's ability to successfully motivate through relationships, words, and actions.

Collaboration Builds Commitment

Over the past years, the debate of commitment over compliance has rocketed forward. While this debate has served us well, the time has come to move forward with implementation, without exception, of gaining commitment. Great leaders seek compliance resulting from commitment, not commitment because of compliance. For a school to ultimately reach the designed vision, mission, and goals, it requires commitment from the stakeholders to plan, implement, maintain, and/or change processes and actions for the cause. The highway to the vision is long and bumpy; therefore, one single person cannot drive the entire route. It takes the collaboration of all stakeholders, committed to the shared vision, to advance the school.

Every stakeholder group, without exception, wants to feel valued and appreciated as a contributing member to the team. Community members, parents, employees, and students all expect their opinions to be heard. Collaboration is actually one of the easiest jobs of the principal; it simply requires planning for the processes, actively listening, and partnering as a team member in shared decision making.

Through collaborative efforts, the principal gains instantaneous buy-in from the stakeholder groups. Ultimately, when there are differences in opinion, the principal will be responsible for finding compromises that do not jeopardize the values of the school. In fact, in advance of any collaborative session, the principal should make the group keenly aware of the overarching vision for the school, which includes the mission and relevant goals.

During any collaborative session, the principal must set forth guidelines for the collaboration. The principal, as contributing member and facilitator, allows everyone's voice to be heard and attempts to move the grouping to a working and purposeful consensus. There should be an outcome of every collaborative session, and like every encounter with any stakeholder, the principal should ensure that every person in the session feels they have worth and dignity when they leave the meeting.

Before leaving any meeting, the principal benefits from tasking the group members to proceed with the charge of making the plan work. Basically, the principal restates dependence on the group for the success of the initiative. Lastly, the principal benefits from a follow-up, in some form, with all contributing members.

Fundamentally, collaboration is a democratic process of the servant-leader. When the leader brings people together in collaboration, the school as a living organism becomes stronger through increased focus and vigor. Through collaboration, all perspectives are explored and consensus typically results. Concerning relationships and actions, Dewey (1916a) wrote, "A being connected with other beings cannot perform his own activities without taking the activities of others into account" (p. 12).

Leaders fearful of bringing stakeholders together in conversation are jeopardizing the effectiveness and efficiency of the organization's present and future success. When the doors are opened and the principal carries stakeholders across the threshold of collaboration, individuals gain increased commitment to the vision of the school.

Authentic Relationships

Visionary principals are dreamers of the Utopian school—one with extraordinary personal growth for all and where organizational expectations are met in a healthy, responsible manner. Taking an idealistic dream of schooling from conceptual to concrete reality demands appreciation and application of leadership's relational components. Effective principals flavor their organization with a sweet saturation of productive relationships while ineffective principals create bitterness and a soured opinion of the school's status. The promise of reaching the school's vision requires authentic relationships between the principals and all stakeholders.

A relationship is an association between two things. Principals, upon appointment to their position, gain hundreds, if not thousands, of immediate relationships with stakeholders. And, with each passing day, more associations are made. Sadly, many principals are not responsive to their stakeholders and never move beyond relationships as association.

Authentic relationships, however, are a priority for the principal as servant-leader. Authentic relationships forge when associated parties become meaningfully real to each other. Through an investment of time together, authentic relationships are built upon understanding of each other, sharing of viewpoints, gaining trust, and cementing a commitment to one another.

Walls (2004) found that successful leaders "build relationships at every opportunity" because they may result in "important collaborations later" (p. 130). The time-consuming process of evolving simple associations into authentic relationships builds an extraordinary tapestry of organizational strength. Wheatley (2002) noted that "when we are together" in authentic relationships, "more becomes possible" (p. 360).

The principalship is a whirlwind of activity, but principals as servant-leaders retain the perspective of authentic relationships throughout the day. They realize that creating and cultivating authentic relationships is key to organizational success. Investing in people, not programs or problems, is a judicious use of time-as-currency for the principal. Hindman,

Seiders, and Grant (2009), wrote that "In a standards-based, accountability-driven context, enhancing relationships may seem like a waste of time" but "The dividends far outweigh any costs" (p. 106).

Authentic relationships bridge gaps and build community within individuals, helping the school thrive. Schools led by principals with association-only relationships are chaotically dysfunctional and figurative street fights among stakeholders are pervasive. In stark contrast, schools led by authentically relational principals have a common vision, discussion of ideas, values-based decision making, higher morale, and greater outcomes for stakeholders.

Barrier walls must be dismantled for schools to be successful. When principals have association-only relationships with stakeholders, the potential of the relationship's impact on organizational improvement is negated. As individuals gain comfort in expression of beliefs and feelings with each other, common ground emerges and ideas for school improvement are sparked. When employees, students, or parents are fearful of open communication with the principal, outcomes are poor. However, servant-leaders are confident enough in their vulnerability to listen and hear dissenting voices, which provide a more holistic perspective of actual reality.

People must feel good about their relationships with the principal and must recognize their voices will be heard. The inclusiveness of servant-leadership, according to Ferch (2004), is "rooted in the far-reaching ideal that people" of all diversities and ideologies "have inherent worth" (p. 226). Even when consensus cannot be reached, or the principal must remain inflexible, people generally appreciate the dialogue, feel respected, and have their dignity validated by the principal.

With every conversation, and every relationship, the principal as servant-leader makes the other person in the relationship feel the most valuable of the two parties. School life is not about the principal; it is about the people and the purpose the principal serves.

Trust is a two-way characteristic required with an authentic relationship. Principals must trust stakeholders and stakeholders must trust principals. Bennis (2002) found that leaders must "generate and sustain trust" to be successful (p. 105). Servant-led organizations are those where individuals trust the competencies of other individuals. Lowe (1998) believes trustworthy leaders and workers "have the ability to perform the tasks" entrusted to them (p. 68).

Trustworthiness develops over-extended periods of time, after successful performances of job-related tasks, and leads to a belief in the abilities of others. The task of building trust and believing in others "requires effort" but is vitally important to the overall success of the leader and organization (Hunter 2004, 107). When trust is broken, there should be effort to mend the relationship; however, principals must consider restraint of communication with repeated breakings of trust. As principal, some relationships cannot be dissolved, but new approaches of association may result in less penetration of vulnerability.

Trust is a mandate of a dynamic, authentic relationship. While trust does not produce a specific outcome for the organization, its presence is a requirement for stakeholders to experience optimal growth and for the organization to function with appropriate fluidity. Clarke (2005) asserts that "All powerful relationships are based on trust and its resulting product, commitment" (p. 17).

As mentioned earlier, principal and stakeholder commitment to the vision, values, mission, and goals of the school is crucially important for the school to increase both its significance and success. Gardiner (1998) believes our future "depends on increasing the level of authentic relationships among human beings" (p. 118). As servant to a better future, principals must take the lead in building, restoring, and creating authentic relationships.

Administrative Teaming

The most professionally intimate relationship, for a school principal, is the relationship with the school's assistant, or vice, principal(s). Highly functioning, symphonic relationship between the administrative leadership team leads to better ideas, cleaner implementation, and reduced stress. Lambert (2002) writes, "A principal who goes it alone or who dominates will find that the school becomes overly dependent on his or her leadership," which weakens the school (p. 40).

Without exception, principals and their assistants must work closely together in a harmonious, vision-seeking manner of distributed leadership. Quality teams force individual members to become more effective, leading to greater capacity within the team itself to reach heightened success.

Wise principals, through reflection, recognize their specific areas of deficit or weakness. From this determination, the hiring of assistants must fill those gaps. If the structure of assistants was already in place, the principal must become aware of specific areas of expertise. Teschke (1996) indicates that principals no longer have to be the "absolute authority" at their schools; but instead, they should share leadership with others who may be better equipped to handling specific issues (p. 1).

School districts, also, are beginning to view the value of assistant principals toward school improvement. In the assistant principal's position description, Seattle Public Schools (2007) claim "The assistant principal's leadership is essential" because "in collaboration and under the supervision of the principal," the assistant principal is "accountable for the continuous growth of students and increased building performance as measured over time by state standards and locally determined indicators" (p. 1).

In their job description of the assistant principal, Phoenix Elementary School District No. 1 (2007) asserts that "The assistant principal assists the site-based principal in the performance of the various leadership responsibilities which are attendant to the successful administration of the school unit" and the assistant principal has the "decision-making authority related to such assignments" determined from collaboration with the school's principal (p. 1). The role of the assistant, or vice, principal is finding more accountability as the value of the position becomes more widely understood and appreciated.

Once the administrative leadership team is established, there must be a clean line of specific responsibility among the group members. These duties form the basis, or foundation, of each member's work. Once the areas of responsibility are determined, it is the principal's job to support and hold accountable all team members for their performance.

The principal should also provide areas of cross-training for the team to learn the work of each other. Cross-training is beneficial in making connections of efficiency throughout the school, building leadership capacity in case of team member absence, and in gaining perspective for shared accountability.

Each week, the administrative leadership team should meet to maintain focus on the vision from a school leadership perspective and coordinate logistical issues from a school-management end. These meetings hold the administrative team accountable to each other, resulting in accountability to the school.

During these sessions, it is important to keep focus on organizational functioning in various areas of schooling and, relatedly, the school's process toward the vision as a result. The atmosphere of these meetings, as set by the principal, must be one of open dialogue and debate as necessary. However, a unified front must exit the closed session for the sake of the school. Few organizational efforts are as important as the weekly meeting of the administrative leadership team.

A strong relationship between members of the administrative leadership team is crucially important. This relationship provides balance for each team member and creates a support structure for tackling difficult situations. Moreover, the benefits of administrative team go beyond the individual team members; the school's total efficiency and effectiveness is impacted.

Professional Learning Community

A school, more than any other established organization, should be a community of learning. It is the responsibility of the principal to develop individuals, thus developing the organization as a whole. Greenleaf (2001) stated a test of the servant-leader is to ask: "Do those served grow as persons? Do they, while being served, become healthier, wiser, freer, more autonomous, more likely themselves to become servants?" (p. 27). If those led by a servant-leader answer "yes" to these questions, then they were developed by the servant-leader.

Servant-leaders understand the importance of professional development and personal growth for others. First, promoting growth shows a commitment to the employee. DeGraaf, Tilley, and Neal (2004) conclude that by "committing to the growth of people," leaders "make a statement that they are in for the long haul, that they are building long-term relationships rather than simply looking for short-term gains" (p. 158).

By nurturing learning and growth, organizations move to heightened levels of success. Melrose (1998) noted, "An environment that encourages personal growth allows the company's most important assets to appreciate in value" (p. 292). Irresponsible principals view teachers as investment capital, or tools, while principals as servant-leaders appreciate teachers as human capital.

The principal accepts responsibility for the development of others as a duty of service. Nakai (2005) found leaders "see enhancing the leadership capability of everyone in their organization as vital to the successful accomplishment of their goals and assuring the lasting viability of their organizations" (p. 214).

The principal sets the tone for continued improvement, or honing, of the learning craft on each campus. An environment of professional learning promotes and expects teachers to advance their skills. It is important to consider that facilitating learning is neither art nor science, in isolation; instead, it is a hybrid of the two. The science of learning takes place in collaboration with other teachers as techniques are discussed, data is analyzed to inform instruction, and curriculum is explored. The art of teaching takes place in the classroom during the implementation of instruction. Basically, the science of teacher preparation creates an artful expression of learning for the teacher and students.

The creation of professional learning communities (PLCs) should not be a separate component of the school. Learning, for students and adults alike, should be the accepted norm. In fact, deviant behavior would be practices noted in students and adults that were in opposition to continuous learning. Dufour, Dufour, Eaker, and Karhanek (2004) believe that "As educators develop their capacity to function as a PLC, they create a culture that stretches the hopes, aspirations, and performance of students and adults alike" (p. 179).

Traditional models of professional development where teachers simply attend workshops have not been effective. Typically, workshops have been the normal method for professional-development attempts. These workshops, historically, have not been specific to needs, preventing the desired level of responsiveness. Furthermore, implementation of information has been faulty with a lack of feedback and follow-through. This haphazard approach has been ineffective and unfortunately turned many educators away from professional growth.

A campus of consistent learning is a more reasonable and effective approach. This requires principals ensuring student learning is taking place through exploration of data, conversations with student learners, and review of relevant artifacts. In relation to teacher improvement, principals should work collaboratively with each teacher to determine areas of strength and areas for refinement.

Logistically, a PLC demands job-embedded learning through shared planning time and freedom to attend relevant off-campus learning sessions where follow-up is a component. Furthermore, teachers are given opportunities to observe other teachers and are willing to have their own classrooms observed with campus-wide teacher-quality improvement as the focus. Additionally, students and teachers need to see their principal modeling similar practices in his or her personal growth.

Celebrate Success

At a school, no accomplishment is too small for celebration. Principals build community, faculty, and student morale in celebration of various accomplishments. Furthermore, by actively celebrating successes, the school's overall culture and spirit is improved.

There are varying degrees of celebrations. These can range from giving a student a congratulatory comment for an accomplishment to a school-wide event to highlight achievement of a major, or vitally important, undertaking. When students achieve a noteworthy accomplishment, win an event, or represent the school well, they deserve recognition.

By providing recognition, the principal validates the student's efforts and sets the stage for further student accomplishments. By doing this, authentic relationships are built. Furthermore, a culture of acknowledging students for minor and major feats should be developed within the school. Too often, the only kind words students receive in a day come from school personnel.

On a larger scale, one basic standard for celebration is the accomplishment of any goal within the vision package. If the goal was important enough to pursue, it is important enough to celebrate its achievement. Celebrations of successes are led by the principal. And, as servant-leader to the stakeholders, the principal is willing to use outside-of-the-box measures for celebration.

The magnitude of the celebration, and corresponding funds needed, are dependent on the accomplishment. Often, community leaders, businesses, and parents are willing to finance celebrations of success. Also, the theme of the celebration should be linked to the accomplishment. As with individual student goals, this validates the importance of the accomplishment and builds an expectation of excellence within the school and community.

Community Partners and Family Involvement

Schools should function as beacons of hope, optimism, and opportunity regardless of the external community of individual home situations of its students. At dismissal, students leave the safe walls of our schools and enter into the *real world*. Enlightened principals create an environment and experiences that, developmentally, prepare students to live, compete, and succeed in the world beyond the school walls. Properly educated students leave school each day with an increased civic, emotional, intellectual, physical, and social awareness. This awareness equips students for overcoming challenges facing them and succeeding in multiple contexts.

To maximize the impact of an education, the principal serves the school, and its students, well by partnering with local community members and businesses to achieve shared goals. Positive gains are the resultant factor when the community is informed of the vision, needs, and basic processes of the school. By involving the community, our access to role models and other resources greatly increases. Furthermore, by informing, involving, and seeking advice from external sources, business leaders are more inclined to support current and future financial needs of the school.

One foundational responsibility of the educational system is to serve families by educating their youth. Each day, across America, families give schools the best they have—their children. They do this with an expectation that the child's time spent at school will be a positive experience and the child will return safely with an increased set of skills. This is the contract principals make with families every day. And, it is a contract that families expect to see honored.

Parents want what is best for their children. This idea of "best" is influenced by the parents' past experiences and current values structure. Despite socioeconomic status, mother and father claws will come out when they perceive their child is being treated unjustly or otherwise wronged. Principals seek to provide the best possible educational opportunities for children, while informing and involving parents when mutually beneficial.

Principals serve families well by honoring the unwritten contract to provide a safe and outstanding education for their children. Furthermore, principals benefit when open communication exists between home and school, which is a basis for the development of authentic relationships. Families are great allies for the schools when educators reach out to partner with this valuable grouping.

[handwritten margin note: School Improvement plan?]

SEVEN

Ethical Leadership

A person educated in mind and not in morals is a menace to society. —
Juanita Kidd Stout

In the late 1960s, Donnie Bickham was a well-rounded and model student at Northwood High School in Louisiana. He was a member of the school's honor society and student council. Furthermore, he was a stand-out athlete in many sports and earned an athletic scholarship to Blinn Junior College in Texas. At Blinn, he continued to excel and was awarded a football scholarship to Baylor University. He was living a noble life and tracked for a lifetime of success.

Sadly, in 1972, he met a tragic and early death as the victim of a head-on collision with a drunken driver on a Texas roadway. He left a positive legacy within his home community, prompting stakeholders to name a school in his honor in 1987. Today, Donnie Bickham Middle School services students in the northern Caddo Parish town of Blanchard.

Unfortunately, during the first two decades of the school's existence, school performance and perception was far from stellar. Donnie Bickham Middle School was not aligned with the excellence of its namesake. In 2007, a native of the local community assumed the helm of the principalship at Donnie Bickham. With a desire to parallel Donnie Bickham Middle School with the legacy of Donnie Bickham himself, Shannon Wall began his work as a transformational leader and servant to the community.

Wall, the principal of Donnie Bickham, speaks highly of his school's namesake. "He was an incredible student-athlete who exhibited leadership skills on a daily basis and excelled in everything he did. In short, he was a model citizen." The principal is a strong believer in neighborhood schools and promises his own children will, one day, attend Donnie Bickham Middle School. He committed, "I won't rest until I believe we're

81

doing all we can to provide the safest and most productive learning environment possible."

Over the last few years, Donnie Bickham has rebirthed itself into a more positive image within the community and academic productivity has followed. The school's performance rating has grown under Wall's leadership. More importantly to Wall, however, is educating students in the likeness of Donnie Bickham. "It is my goal to create 650 little Donnie Bickhams here on our campus," he said. "Donnie Bickham was the type of person who felt a strong connection to his school, he connected to his community, he excelled as an individual, he was never greater than his team, he was loyal, and he was an exceptional role model."

Wall views the reculturing of Donnie Bickham Middle School as a moral battle for the future lives of his students and the quality of his local community. "We have begun educating our students about Donnie Bickham in hopes that they might take the challenge to live their lives the way that Donnie led his," said Wall. "We have also begun recognizing the top students at every grade level for exhibiting academic and extracurricular traits that Donnie exhibited."

Accepting the responsibility to ethically develop the students under his care, Wall has become the second face of Donnie Bickham. "I truly believe that our work could transform our community into something extraordinarily special and my goal is to leave this place better than I found it," Wall said. According to student-performance data, enrollment numbers, and positive perceptions of the school, Wall is already achieving his goals.

Donnie Bickham would be proud of the school's transformation toward excellence. However, as a competitor, he would be encouraging the school to zestfully become greater and grow stronger as a team of stakeholders. Wall, as the school's leader, is responsible for bringing Donnie Bickham Middle School to levels of greatness that correspond with its namesake—Donald "Donnie" Thomas Bickham. So far, he is doing a fine job.

STANDARD #5

> An education leader promotes the success of every student by acting with integrity, fairness, and in an ethical manner.

Democratic Mindedness

While individuals are captive to various forms of constraint, the inner soul of each person seeks freedom. The early European colonists to the Americas made the dangerous voyage across the ocean for different reasons; however, they shared a quest for, and belief in, a better life. As families settled and towns developed, individuals desired to govern themselves in an American way and decided to formally disconnect from Mother England's rule. This rebellious decision for independence led to a war between the colonists and the British Empire, which became known as the American Revolution.

During this Revolutionary War, British soldiers were sent to the Americas to regain control of the rebellious colonists. These English red-coats were better financed and trained. However, despite the obvious financial and military advantage of the British, they could not overcome the American spirit for independence. Fighting with resolute purpose, the Americans cast the sword of freedom into the heart of English control. With the retreat of the British, the colonists earned something with malleability, potential, and purity—they held *opportunity* for an American dream.

An educational system emerged as a necessary component of American life. Initial access to formal education was restricted but, over time, it has become cemented as a right for every American, regardless of demographic. Today, struggles for democracy in education still exist. Democratic-minded educators must seek to eliminate inequality and injustice in educational practices and policies.

Every child deserves an outstanding education, rich with opportunities for civil, emotional, intellectual, physical, spiritual, and social growth. Through educative experiences, children mature into healthy, knowledgeable, and satisfied contributors to society. Fundamental American ideology supports society providing an education for the child in hopes of the individual, in adulthood, giving back to society through citizenship and economics.

At the campus level, principals as servant-leaders recognize sound schooling as a democratic ideal. These leaders seek to provide democratic practices within the school's policies and practice while preparing students to act democratically in American society. Democracy is the foundational fabric of daily American life. A democratically minded principal, in service to freedom, recognizes that democracy is a process, not a product.

It is erroneous to believe America is fully democratic with antidemocratic practices running prevalent in daily life and public policy. School principals must provide for environments and opportunities where all stakeholders are involved in a democratic quest. It is antidemocratic, however, for a leader not to actively and systemically lead an effort to increase democratic practices within the school and society.

Unfortunately, democracy has fallen on hard times in educational settings. The benefits of democracy in schools are countless, but too few principals are democratically minded. In an accountability era, a primary concern is the elevation of standardized test scores. It is unhealthy to Americanism for principals to set democracy aside in a zealous attempt to improve test performance. With a loss of democratic awareness, principals have inadvertently sold the soul of every student into the slavery of the oppressed.

Democratic-mindedness is the skill of keeping democracy at the forefront of all consideration and action, seeking for the pursuit of full democracy to be preserved for future generations. Effective principals question every school initiative, policy, and practice in terms of its benefit or detriment to increasing democracy within the school. Standardized test scores will rise by giving voice to all, sharing decision making among all, examining equality among all, and making each student's education an individualized experience facilitated by effective teachers. As the young citizenry grows civically healthier, America becomes stronger.

Principals must ensure the training of students concerning the story of the American nation, what it means to be democratic, how to act in a democracy, and the importance of our democracy. Without the active embedding of fundamental training, the future of the nation's democratic status is jeopardized. The history of the world cites numerous examples of crumbling nations as the citizenry took their democracies for granted. In recent history, the horrid dictatorship of Adolf Hitler was spawned from a nation that lost sight of democracy.

America must teach democracy to retain democracy and, like so many things, the responsibility rests with the school principal. Goodlad, Bromley, and Goodlad (2004) found that "Democracy is a daunting work in progress that should never be taken for granted" because nothing "says it will exist fifty years from now or, for that matter, until next week" (p. 35). Principals cannot allow democratic freedom to crumble for the sake of other interests. Without pushing a democratic agenda, a principal as servant-leader has failed in potential to recreate the American dream for future generations.

Spirituality

Individuals select professional vocations for personal reasons, but sometimes their work selects them. This notion forms the basis that principals are *called* to their position as a mission of influence and service. Enlightened principals accept the calling and create conditions for significant success in the lives of stakeholders. By doing this work, struggling through daily challenges, and overcoming adversity, principals answer their calling. To the contrary, ineffective principals become disconnected with purpose after losing service.

Spirituality in leadership is a core belief of connectivity to a calling, power, or source larger than life itself. Through this connection of faith, the leader embraces self as an instrument for helping others in their daily life and connecting them to their calling. Spirituality requires overcoming darkness (such as envy, greed, hatred, and self-edification) to achieve the purity of graciousness, humility, and service. Efforts to become spiritual require values clarification for the leader to realize the important beliefs of life, such as placing the needs of others ahead of personal endeavors.

The spiritual framework for servant-leadership is more than two thousand years old through the example of Jesus Christ, the Biblical Son of God. A few years before His death, Jesus selected a grouping of twelve ordinary men to teach in the ways of goodness and preparation to extend His message beyond death. During their time with Jesus, these disciples saw numerous examples of service to mankind and they grew to recognize Him as the Son of God.

The life of Jesus, in itself, is the most remarkable example of servant-leadership imaginable. Before His death, Jesus and the disciples shared a meal together. During this Last Supper, the leader of the men took a cloth, which belted His waist, and water from a basin and began washing the feet of the disciples. To place this in perspective, one must understand that feet were considered a filthy part of the body.

Confused, a disciple is uncomfortable with his leader doing such a disgusting task. Jesus responds by telling them, "If I then, your Lord and teacher, have washed your feet, you also ought to wash one another's feet" as "I have given you an example that you should do as I have done to you." Jesus, as Son to the creator of the Universe, essentially proclaims that no position of authority is too elite to serve others first.

In Christian belief, Jesus dies on a cross for the sins of man. Ultimately, He ascends to be with His Father God in Heaven. In terms of servant-leadership, there is nothing more powerful than the example provided by the death, burial, and resurrection of Jesus so that others may have their sins forgiven and, eventually, live an eternal life in Heaven.

Although the story of Jesus is an example of servant-leadership, spirituality does not require religion. Instead, personal spirituality seeks authenticity toward the call to lead in a manner worthy of the position. As seen in the life of Jesus, service was more than words; it was action. In education, leadership becomes spiritual as the principal's values are truly understood and are practiced with fidelity.

Leadership character develops as the principal habitually practices tasks of service to others with integrity to core values. Doohan (2007) writes that "Spiritual leadership is not something you add on to an already existing leadership style; rather it permeates everything that one does" and "The best leaders are the ones who are grounded in motivating values and have faith" (p. 282).

An old adage states, "Your talk talks and your walk talks. But, your walk talks louder than your talk talks." While somewhat hard to express, the above phrase captures the idea of being authentic to values as a leader. Duffy (2003) writes that, "If there is a difference between what you say your values are and the values actually expressed in your behavior, people will believe what they see, not what they hear come out of your mouth or see in your written memorandum" (p. 23).

With a number of hypocritical behaviors being exposed daily and questions surrounding the authenticity of leaders, it has become increasingly important to be a true authentic, or to be real. To succeed at being real, leaders must participate in what Begley (2001) calls "a thoughtful and rigorous analysis of leadership activity" (p. 354) to examine their behaviors in a quest for authenticity.

yes!

There are few things more discrediting than hypocrisy. A principal as hypocrite is one who talks a certain way and acts another, leading to extreme distrust and poor levels of effectiveness. Hypocrisy usually arises through a lack of critical reflection into one's practice as a leader, or from leadership practice not being directly tied to humanistic values such as care, democracy, fairness, and social justice.

LEARN FROM MISTAKES

Leadership, however, lends itself to mistakes. The spiritual leader accepts fault and learns from mistakes. Sokolow (2002) cautioned that "Enlightened leaders are not infallible" as "They make errors as we all do, but they are growing and continually learning from their experiences" (p. 34).

Spiritual leaders accept the call and responsibility to serve. With this acceptance, they seek to find their way in making the world, or even their schools, a better place for humanity. Through spirituality, the principal as servant-leader maintains congruency between espoused values and values-in-use. Resulting from the inner desire for goodness and the outward expression of service, spirituality in leadership is attained.

Reflectivity and Reflexivity

The inner peace that spirituality provides comes from the satisfaction of one's leadership actions matching core values and the improvement of life for others. Servant-leaders are fulfilled by watching others achieve and mature as a result of their relationship. However, for continual improvement, servant-leaders must refine their practice. Principals as servant-leaders use a process of *reflectivity* and *reflexivity* to increase their effectiveness.

Reflectivity is a process in which one views his or her practices from a personal approach. Deconstructing reflectivity, Killion and Todnem (1991) define three types of reflection as *reflection-in-practice, reflection-of-practice*, and *reflection-for-practice*.

Reflection-in-practice takes place during the event. This process of thinking is very reactive to the specific situation and is based on past experiences and the specific context of the situation.

Reflection-of-practice is thinking about an event after it happened. This postevent process allows the individual to replay the event and appreciate a better understanding of exactly what took place. Both reflection-in-practice and reflection-of-practice are positive attributes for a leader. These two processes, alone, are not enough for reaching heightened levels of reflection.

Moving a step further than the practices above, the servant-leader participates in a proactive process called *reflection-for-practice*. During this process, the individual learns from the event to improve future situations. Effective school leaders, according to Jenlink (2010), "allow their critical reflections upon their practice to inform theory" (p. 205). The theory of the scholar-practitioner-leader consists of knowledge and skills to improve future practice.

With reflectivity consuming time, it is important to make it worthwhile. As a goal of reflection, the practices of principals in future situations should improve. According to Hatton and Smith (1995), reflection is "deliberate thinking about action, with a view for its improvement" (p. 40). *Reflection-for-practice* is the only process that seeks continual improvement for the servant-leader.

An extension of reflectivity is a process of reflexivity. In reflexivity, individuals consider how others view their practice and actions. It is an act of considering the personality and values of another person, or group, and stepping inside their psyche to view oneself. This spiritual journey transcends the pragmatism of reflection and requires skills of awareness, perception, and vulnerability. For a servant-leader, however, it is critical to understand how others view one's actions, approach, position, or stance.

When leaders understand how they are viewed, they become more capable in their role. This appreciation allows the leader to alter or reinforce practices on behalf of the organizational purpose. Through reflexive practice, leaders keep followers. Translated for the servant-leader, the leader's opportunity to serve is renewed. A servant-leader without a team is not much of a leader.

Ethic of Care

> Our world has become a large, impersonal, busy institution. We are alienated from each other. Although crowded, we are lonely. Distant. Pushed together but uninvolved. No longer do most neighbors visit across the backyard fence. The well-manicured lawn is the modern moat that keeps barbarians at bay. Hoarding and flaunting have replaced sharing and caring. It's like we are occupying common space but have no common interests, as if we're on an elevator with rules like: "No talking, smiling, or eye contact without written consent of management." Painful though it may be for us to admit here in the great land of America, we're losing touch with one another. The motivation to help, to encourage, yes, to serve our fellow man is waning. . . . And yet, it is these things that form the essentials of a happy and fulfilled life. (Swindoll 2001, 96)

The preceding quote sets a discomforting atmosphere, illuminating fundamental concerns regarding the state of our society and its schools. Americans, too often, have distanced themselves from others, and this separation is mirrored in our educational institutions by its impersonal policies, faculty, and students.

Under the current definition of school accountability, educational leaders are responsible for improving initiatives deemed top priority. However, a new dialogue must be accepted where stakeholders have an obligation to genuinely give and willingly accept care with hopes of a new, more personal and compassionate definition of accountability is accepted.

Student learning must be the focus of every school; however, a more inclusive culture of moral, social, psychological, and spiritual enlightenment is promoted to augment learning. In our fast-paced culture, everyone is trying to keep up, and the individual and personal needs of stakeholders are being omitted from the curriculum. Sadly, the primary complaint of students as found in several research studies is that their teachers *don't care* about them. Principals as servant-leaders provide a clear message that an ethic of caring toward one another is the norm.

A primary challenge of integrating care within schools is finding a working definition for the term. Stockdale and Warelow (2000) realize this priority by writing, "Although society has broad understanding and various meanings of care, there is no single definition that is applicable to all situations" and that "rather than trying to define the concept," educators should "try and interpret it" (p. 1258). It is a human quality and a moral disposition that is both inherent and necessary for being human, building community, and living democratically.

An ethic of care is an orientation of connectedness, as part of an authentic relationship, where we share genuine concern, elicit both empathy and sympathy, and promote hopeful solutions to assist ones in need. Care is preventative and responsive, passive and aggressive, happy and sad. Care is what it needs to be, when it needs to be, how it needs to be. Care is an age-old, yet revolutionary, practice.

Envisioning and practicing an ethic of care will create greater feelings of security, comfort, and accomplishment in individual students, thus transforming the whole school. To accept care as a solution to confusion within American schools requires courage from the educational leader, moving past traditional school practices. Noddings (1992) wrote that many educators believe they can "improve education merely by designing a better curriculum, finding and implementing a better form of instruction, or instituting a better form of classroom management" (p. 173).

These desires alone will fall short of education's ultimate possibility. Through creating an atmosphere of care, principals will notice students and faculty more encouraged, conscientious, compassionate, and serving. Care reproduces servant-leadership among all stakeholders.

The hope for an ethic of care within a school lies within the hands of the principal. Leaders have the greatest capacity and authority to encourage, promote, and achieve positive change for the benefit of all stakeholders. Marzano, Waters, and McNulty (2005) wrote that "Leadership is critical to the success of any institution or endeavor" (p. 4). Revolutionary educational leaders must cast aside the nets of impersonal sameness and become eclectic fishers of individual student needs, goals, and desires.

For the principal, care for others must be prevalent practice, genuine in approach, and manifested within the school's atmosphere. Being a caring leader is not an event; instead, it is a way of life. As servant-leaders to people, principals eradicate schools of institutionalism and provide a culture where burdens are shared, consideration is given, and selfishness is replaced with selflessness.

Social Justice

When all citizens appropriately share the benefits of Americanism, social justice is achieved. In education, schools must provide equality of experience for all stakeholders. Johnson, according to Dupuis, Musial, Hall, and Gollnick (1999), "Any structures or practices that interfere with the simultaneous goals of equity and excellence, that perpetuate preexisting social and economic inequities, are subject to critique and elimination,"(p. 149). This quote is appropriate; however, principals must consider more than "equity and excellence." Equality and inclusiveness must be priority.

Too often, principals fall into the trap of equity-only practice. In this context, equity means providing sameness throughout the stakeholders. Although this is a safe approach for principals, it marginalizes the growth of faculty and students. This concept is easiest to understand if a teaching example is considered. If an instructor presents the entire class the same objective in the same way, this is equity. However, some students are naturally advanced beyond this learning objective and will be bored, some students are on-target with needing this objective, and some students are intellectually below this objective and will not understand.

If asked, the teacher could insist that everyone was treated equally; thus equity was provided. However, the approach marginalized the learning of both advanced and lower-level learners, meaning equality of education was not provided. The advanced learners would have benefitted from extensions from the objective while the lower-level learners needed more scaffolding of knowledge to better understand. An astute principal addresses these types of issues with teachers to promote effectiveness and efficiency in learning.

Instead of providing absolute sameness, the principal as servant-leader is critically aware of diverse needs. And, for the principal, alienation is created when school operations are not appropriate for the particular individuals. The resources provided must match the needs of the people.

For consideration, assume a principal establishes a professional development session for faculty on classroom management procedures. Teachers having high levels of student engagement and low levels of inappropriate classroom behaviors do not need this training. Their time is too valuable to be insulted with equity. But, for the principal, it is just easier to say "everyone must attend." In this instance, social justice is denied as equality of professional development is not provided to the teachers. Effective teachers match resources to needs.

Social justice requires principals to consider the decisions, initiatives, policies, and practices of the school and determine their appropriateness toward either advancing or marginalizing each stakeholder. Again, as a theme of the principalship, differentiation of thought and action is required with servant-leadership. When principals consider outcomes for individuals, instead of simply the masses, social justice is more likely to be achieved. Practices that minimize, marginalize, or otherwise prevent full humanitarianism are unacceptable to a servant-leader of people.

Educational Grace

A world of people is a world of mistakes. At schools, principals continuously deal with mistakes. Examples include students doing poorly on assignments, teachers forgetting their duty post, and parents irrationally justifying the misbehavior of their *do-no-wrong* children. Even principals, especially because of their busyness and magnitude of work, are especially prone to mistakes.

Principals, because of positional authority, are often placed in the role of judge, jury, and executioner when expectations are not met. Depending on the severity of the mistake, these are the occasions when *going to the principal's office* is not a comfortable experience. Figuratively, principals hold the lives of others in their hands each day and have the opportunity to sentence guilty parties. Before laying the hammer down, principals should consider the redemptive and corrective impact of grace.

John Newton was an English sailor in the 1700s. Although he received an early education and several noble jobs, the darkness of his heart overcame goodness. His corruptive behavior during the time of slave trade was so despicable that he became detested by other sailors. His words were blasphemous, his character was vile, and his actions were deplorable.

In 1748, he was sailing aboard the merchant ship *Greyhound* when a fierce storm erupted on the waters. During this danger, the boat was whipped around aimlessly at sea and began filling with water. As hope faded and an ocean grave seemed imminent, the vulnerable Newton called upon God for safety. Within time, the storm ceased and Newton's life was renewed through a contract of commitment with God. From that experience, Newton penned the following lyrics:

> Amazing Grace, how sweet the sound
> That saved a wretch like me
> I once was lost but now am found,
> Was blind but now I see

Newton believed he was spared by God's grace. For this, his life and his actions gradually shifted in a new direction. Newton learned from his experience and, resultantly, made a positive impact on the world. In a connection to the principalship, Vaszauskas (2005) believes, "Educational grace means that we should never write off a student" as their potential for greatness is unforeseen (p. 60).

The enlightened principal views mistakes as opportunities for growth in recognition of each individual's incompleteness. Philosophically, the essence of a person is the sum of who they have yet to become. When stakeholders are viewed in terms of potential for contribution, instead of solely based on previous actions, a more graceful construct of leadership is being practiced.

The approach of grace does not eliminate the need for consequence; moreover, grace expounds upon the impact of the consequence by making it relational between the guilty individual and the principal. Grace turns the application of a consequence into a meaningful educative experience whereas the principal seeks meaning, counsels, advises, enforces, and teaches. Throughout the process, the principal ensures that the erring stakeholder maintains dignity as a human with potential for significance and success in life.

In the busy lives of principals, it is easiest to enforce a consequence and move on. A *This is what you did* and *This is the penalty* approach is not beneficial for anyone and rarely prevents future inappropriate behavior. A better investment of time calls for the principal to listen and clarify how the behavior is unaligned with the values of the school.

Grace does not, and should not, usurp the power of policy; however, it calls for erring on the side of care, democracy, and social justice. And, yes, flexibility of rules is graceful when the flexibility does not negatively impact others and leads to a more positive future outcome for even one person.

Educational grace is not a weak approach to school leadership; instead, it is a reflective process of time investment, teaching of expectations, and relationship building. In the words of Ghandi, "The weak can never forgive" as "Forgiveness is the attribute of the strong." When people recognize they are in trouble, it sets a perfect tone for principals to show humanity and forge a relationship. There is great power in saying *I know what you did . . . It is not right . . . But, I believe in your ability to learn from this mistake and for us to move forward.* Few principals will lose sleep over giving second chances and erring on the side of a student or teacher.

Positional authority of the principalship provides an opportunity to use *power over* people. According to Sergiovanni (1987), "Power over is concerned with dominance, control, and hierarchy" (p. 122). Instead, servant-leaders use the *power to* change, influence, and mold the lives of others through their positional authority.

As a component of service, grace provides an outstanding example of humanity to all stakeholders. Vaszauskas (2005) wrote, "Grace is a gift, free of charge, unexpected, undeserved" and "No gift is needed in return; it is absolutely unconditional" (p. 57). A responsibility of leadership is to ensure positive future outcomes. The principal as servant-leader uses educational grace as a method for shaping lives and making a positive difference.

EIGHT

Political Leadership

Education is the most powerful weapon which you can use to change the world. — Nelson Mandela

Urban in culture and disadvantaged in demographic, Ryan Elementary has every reason to be a failure. With 98 percent of students labeled economically poor, the Baton Rouge school could supply a litany of excuses. In our educational system, it would not be abnormal for this school to be a failure. In fact, it would be easier to simply write off this public school or hand it over to a charter operation. However, Darlene Brister, the school's principal, selected a different approach. And it worked.

"The job of an educational leader is not easy in any school; however, the role of an educational leader in a failing school is more critical than most," said Brister, a thirteen-year veteran principal. "Schools such as Ryan require a courageous leader and my mission has been to harness the energy released through this conflict in order to mobilize the entire community to discover solutions for problems and become advocates for change." And changed the school has.

Over the past decade, the school has seen an approximate 40 percent increase in academic performance as measured by standardized testing. These results have earned Ryan Elementary such honors as being a National Blue Ribbon School and a Louisiana High Performance, High Poverty award winner. For the principal, she has been named a Louisiana Principal of the Year and was even awarded the Key to the City by the mayor.

This spectacular increase in school performance, and the awards it garnered, did not happen by chance. Instead, the success has been achieved by a school outlining and striving to achieve a vision for learning. The stakeholders know the specific vision for the school and are held accountable for their actions. When that vision is threatened, the principal safeguards and advocates for her school. In consideration of the principal, a faculty member said, "Mrs. Brister is proactive in her efforts to change and improve Ryan Elementary and is always testing the limits in an effort to change things" because "Her decisions are in the best interests of students."

Notably, Mrs. Brister enters the political arena for her school and its students. She believes she is the voice for the voiceless. "There are constant challenges to improve student achievement and I continually fight for our students based upon our platform of beliefs to improve and achieve excellence," Brister shared. Specifically, she has advocated regarding budgets, school calendars, superintendent hiring, textbook adoption, resource allocation, and implementation of new district initiatives. With each battle, she has kept the vision of the school and the needs of the students at the forefront.

She understands her political endeavors are not always popular. "In my courageous leadership role, I have had to step outside of the box and take chances that I felt would move our school forward," Brister stated. "Even though many of my decisions and ideas were met with resentment, I have continued to confront adversity head on for the sake of improving student achievement." In working with this principal, a belief that all students will learn at Ryan Elementary is easily noticeable.

Mrs. Brister has done an outstanding job at Ryan Elementary. A school many viewed as hopeless was provided with a vision, opportunity, and a public advocate for its success. With this, the school has responded positively with sustained improvement. The stakeholders of Ryan Elementary adopted the motto of *Every Child, Every Day, Whatever It Takes*. And, that same drive is present within the being of their courageous leader—an advocate for student learning and Ryan Elementary named Darlene Brister.

STANDARD #6

An education leader promotes the success of every student by understanding, responding to, and influencing the political, social, economic, legal, and cultural context.

Authority and Power

The integration of authority and power starts with a choice to accept a position of school principal. Greenleaf (1977) states "The servant-leader is a servant first" and "It begins with the natural feeling that one wants to serve," then, "Conscious choice brings one to aspire to lead" (p. 27).

In the practice of servant-leadership, one must be considerate of the role and relationship between authority and power. With the mention of servant-leadership, questions about authority and power frequently arise. It is important for principals to continually heighten their understanding and sensitivity to the dynamic between these two forces because both are crucial to success as a servant-leader in the twenty-first century.

Both authority and power are necessary for action. Unfortunately, they have received negative connotations as some leaders became ruthlessly authoritative or recklessly powerful. Students study these leaders in history books each day; moreover, adults see misuses of authority and power in the news media. Because of these negative examples, some individuals completely shy away from the taboo mention of power or authority. For a purposeful, responsible, and useful interplay to exist, a basic understanding of their value is required.

Principals receive authority when formally placed in the position as the school's leader. From an organizational standpoint, this cannot be escaped. Someone has to be the official leader of the school with the rights to act, speak, and write as the voice of the school. Positional authority is required for certain responsibilities and duties of the principalship to be achieved. The beauty of authority for the servant-leader is that it provides a vehicle for influence.

Because of authority, the principal has the right to ensure democratic practices, an ethic of care, social justice, and overall school effectiveness. As the site-based leader, the principal utilizes local context, creating an atmosphere of civic, intellectual, physical, and social learning.

Power for the servant-leader is influence. Legendary basketball Coach John Wooden believes "A leader has a most powerful influence on those he or she leads" and considers the responsibility of leadership "a sacred trust" between the servant-leader and the stakeholders. As a role-model educator, principals gain appreciation from the stakeholders.

By treating people fairly and acting responsibly in the best interest of the organization's people and purpose, principals build trust. Through preparation, research, and intelligence, principals receive credibility. As these relational qualities develop, servant-leaders are able to empower others to do more, achieve more, and be more. With stakeholders seeking a collective vision and the principal utilizing authentic relationships, positive outcomes become prevalent.

Principals must maintain humility in their personal lives and professional position. With an attitude that reflects core values and wisdom supported by a democratic ethic, principals stay grounded in their work of helping others and achieving organizational significance and success. The application, by the leader, of both authority and power is a form of communication. Enomoto and Kramer (2007) believe "Only if communication is open, sharing, and grounded in truth-seeking, can we begin to form social structures that can handle the diverse needs of our societies" (p. 84).

Principals confident in their ability to positively shape a school and its stakeholders are desired. These principals, through their authority, distribute leadership (not just tasks) to others, building growth capacity within the organization. Furthermore, these principals utilize power as the ability to influence others toward actions and decisions that draw the school closer to a determined vision.

With relationships built on genuine sincerity, trust, and a belief in one another, principals never have to say *I'm the principal and do it because I said so*. Instead, stakeholders recognize the principal's humble status and respond because of shared responsibility for doing the right thing for the sake of the school's human interests.

With their formal position of authority, principals are provided an outstanding opportunity to empower others through positive influence, or power. Duffy (2003) wrote that "To make a real difference, leaders in school districts must be able to affect decisions and events" (p. 14). Schools need to be led by effective principals, authority must be accepted by the principal, and power should translate to positive influence on the lives of stakeholders. Principals should use their authority and power wisely.

Cultural Awareness

There is an overuse of the term *culture* in American society without regard to its actual meaning. Each day, people espouse comments about *cultural sensitivity, cultural correctness, cultural tolerance, cultural diversity*, and even *pop culture*. However, these comments are out of context or lacking a true understanding of their root nature within the term *culture*.

Macionis (1997) defines *culture* as "The values, beliefs, behavior, and material objects that constitute a people's way of life" (p. 62). It is the way we think and act which provides a bridge to the past and a guide to our future.

There is both material and nonmaterial culture. Items of material culture are the tangible things created by members of a society such as cars, houses, and computers. A society's nonmaterial culture includes the intangible world of ideas created by members of a society, which should include democracy, social justice, and an ethic of care.

Typically, communal and societal cultures have a significant impact on the cultures within the local schools. But, even beyond location, each school has a distinct cultural identity. There is no way to fully understand a culture of a school without being immersed into its five research-based components: symbols, language, values, norms, and material objects (Macionis 1997).

School principals, especially when newly appointed to their post, make mistakes stemming from a lack of cultural awareness. These mistakes, when made, are detrimental to the leaders' credibility in relation to authenticity and sensitivity.

For the principal, cultural awareness is a critical understanding and appreciation for the existing components of the school's culture. Beyond that, however, the servant-leader possesses a desire and plan for shifting the school toward heightened levels of academic and humanistic excellence with its vision in mind.

A principal learns the existing culture of the school through observation and experience. With this knowledge, an appreciation of the school's unique cultural significance is gained. As an understanding of existing culture is solidified, the principal seeks to rectify anything culturally dichotomous with the school's vision. Hampton (2010) believes "An organization dedicated to reculturing examines current practices through a critical lens and seeks to establish new cultures that represent diversity, social justice, and democracy" (p. 188).

Attempts to challenge the status quo, existing mindsets, or prevailing practices are often met with fervent resistance. People hold an innate inflexibility toward change. However, when reculturing is aligned with values and overall school vision, the principal must facilitate the process. Duffy (2003) found "If this immune system can be unlocked and modified, people can then release new energy on behalf of new ways of seeing and being" and this "exists at the critical core of leadership for systemic change." Altering cultures of ineffectiveness or dehumanization requires the principal to work within, not behind or ahead of, the change process. Furthermore, the leader must be courageous to overcome attempts to cease progression.

As servant to the school, the principal empowers others to assist in any reculturing efforts. Marinho (2005) believes "It is not so much about charisma, as it is about capacity, the competence, in complex societies, to point direction, motivate, accept divergence and convince" others of a better way than the existing culture (p. 121).

Together, the team implements structures that make the school, as a system, more acceptable as a democratic hub for learning where students and teachers thrive and mature. With a democratic school organization, stakeholders learn how such values as democracy and diversity can be implanted within the school as well as their lives beyond the school walls (Starratt 2001).

Power of the People

Contrary to history lessons or personal beliefs, America is not fully democratic. In fact, democracies do not exist anywhere on Earth. Although America was founded on democratic principles, it has yet to arrive at full realization. And despite how negative this sounds, it is actually acceptable in the context of democracy as a quest.

Democracy will never be achieved in terms of a product; instead, it is a process seeking the promise of its reality. This adventure is one that desires practices where majority opinion is accepted and minority view is not oppressed. Democracy is about living together, honoring one another's humanity, and being civically responsible. In a democracy, everyone's voice is heard, no member is marginalized by a system or another member, and peace is upon the land.

The origins of this way of life came from the Greeks, the hands that rocked the cradle of democracy. Their *demokratia* was a new method of living, a more inclusive approach to life. Deconstruction of the term democracy reveals *demos* meaning *people* and *kratos* meaning *power*. When coupled, democracy actually means power of the people.

True democracy is more than a form of government; it is the power of the people to construct a life worth living communally with others. Goodlad, Bromley, and Goodlad (2004) found that "Democracy, first and foremost, is a shared way of life" that "begins with who we are as individuals and the relationships we have with those around us, and it radiates outward from that center to encompass all of humanity" (p. 82).

For the school principal, democracy means creating an atmosphere and experiences where stakeholders associate harmoniously, advancing toward the vision of the school. Dewey (1916b) stated that educational leaders must "remember that they above all others are consecrated servants of the democratic ideas in which alone this country is truly a distinctive nation" (p. 210).

The principal saturates the school with democratic dialogue, action, and reflection. Regarding democracy in schools, Hampton (2010) wrote, "Educational leaders must facilitate this desire through the creation of an equitable environment that not only discusses the need to include all stakeholders, but ensur[es] this desire through inclusionary action" (p. 187).

Ultimately, students leave the school system. Hopefully, they are armed with a diploma and the skills needed to provide an adequate standard of living. Furthermore, however, students must leave school with an understanding of how to live civically in society. They must, through their school experience, appreciate their responsibility to productively contribute to our society through paying taxes, serving others, and informed voting. It is a tragic injustice for students to exit American schools without a sense of the rights and responsibilities of actually being an American.

The democratic work of the principal goes beyond school environment and experiences to include personal commitment. The principal as servant-leader acts as a role-model of democratic character, which highlights a way of life that is virtuous and honorable. The principal leads a transparent life, comparable to living in a glass house, which provides an example to stakeholders.

As a human, the principal is not perfect; instead, the leader's imperfections are recognized through self-reflection and critical examination, which fosters personal and professional growth. The principal seeks to be a better person, and leader, tomorrow than he or she is today—this is a vow of service.

Criticalist Bricoleur

Despite characterizations to the contrary, the work of the principal is far from dull. Most anyone who has trailed, or job-shadowed, a principal at work will attest to the principal's constant absorption into matters of the school. As principals work in both proactive and responsive ways, they must remain true in their first calling of service while promoting democratic practices. As a part of organizational life, principals readily recognize problems and must overcome for the sake of all stakeholders.

As a matter of attitude, however, servant-leaders consider these challenges as *opportunities*. Jenlink (2005) believes school leaders are "charged with a public responsibility to education" and they engage "in intellectual work with the purpose, in large part, to create educative spaces wherein future generations may learn the knowledge and skills necessary to build a principled and democratic society" (p. 3). As a dutiful leader, principals as servant-leaders are responsible to overcome adversity without regard to personal interest or need.

When approaching *opportunities* for refinement or improvement, servant-leaders seek solutions. No doubt, when situations arise, some individuals will attempt overcomplication of solutions, which is typically unnecessary. With time as currency, the servant-leaders use a pragmatic response. Pragmatism, according to the *American Heritage Dictionary* , is a "matter of fact way of approaching or assessing situations or of solving problems" (p. 1378).

As a beautiful approach to logical thinking and life, pragmatism is a suitable manner for resolution. Cherryholmes (1999) wrote that pragmatists "look for results" (p. 4). The servant-leader, as a pragmatist, seeks outcomes that are both effective for the organization and humanistic for the people.

Pragmatism pairs itself well with the role of a *bricoleur.* In France, a bricoleur is a "handyman or handywoman who makes use of the tools available to complete a task" (Kincheloe 2001, 680). As principals seek resolutions for issues, they consider all resources available, acting as a pragmatic bricoleur. In this capacity, principals as bricoleurs explore available capital and human talents, both internal and external to the school, to get results aligning with the organizational vision, values, mission, and goals.

Principals identify the issue causing a glitch or disruption, determine the causes, and select a more appropriate, or desired, outcome. As a pragmatic bricoleur, utilizing all available resources, the servant-leader seeks a better result for the stakeholders of the organization in the simplest way.

William of Occam, a premedieval philosopher-scientist, believed the simplest solution of competing theories for correction, was the best. This approach was coined as Occam's Razor or the Law of Parsimony. Ubben, Hughes, and Norris (2007) found "The importance is that given two or more choices, when data are available, the simplest solution is frequently the best solution" and "This is a common-sense warning again unnecessarily complicated solutions, especially to practice problems" (p. 56).

With this information, the principal uses reflection, academic preparation, and common sense to identify possible solutions with the pros and cons of each. From the possible solutions available, the principal selects the solution with simplistic implementation, democratic impact, and the one with the greatest opportunity for successful correction of the initial issue. These results, however, must be aesthetically desirable, satisfying, and harmonious. The principal doesn't overexcite or turn decision making into a dramatic process; instead, with an even temper and lucidity, the principal brings peace and calmness to the school so learning processes may continue with normalcy.

Influencing Systems

The nature of leadership requires individuals able and committed to achieve something, make life better, or improve a process. Without hope for a better way, leadership would simply seek sustainment. This notion lies in opposition to American optimism. Seeing leaders as the individuals who prosper a group or organization is vital to understanding their potential for changing systems beyond the school level. Duffy (2003) wrote that "Influence is the essence of leadership" (p. 21).

There are problems within the national, state, and local educational systems. Anyone who has experienced the bureaucratic machines of formal education can recite a litany of concerns. The principal as servant-leader seeks to influence the larger system through advocacy improvement.

There are three levels of leadership influence (Gardner 1995). Ordinary principals relate the traditional story of schooling as effectively as possible and they do not seek to improve a system toward finding better ways. Innovative principals take the traditional story of school and bring new attention or a fresh twist to leadership; however, their efforts are not typically systemic. Visionary principals are not content to accept the current practices of schooling, and they change systems to create new stories.

Visionary principals are advocates for their schools and the stakeholders they serve. With an unwavering passion to improve systems, these principals are involved at all levels of government, hoping to influence the system. The system of education influences the outcomes for students. With this knowledge, it is not considered radical for principals to advocate for their stakeholders; instead, it is the responsibility of caring principals to influence change. Bourgeois (2010) argued that "Working as a change agent, this leader seeks to correct past wrongs, empowering all to reach greater values and awareness" (p. 242).

As advocates, principals are keenly aware of their responsibility to improve systems. Using knowledge of processes, relationship-building, and a zest for finding better ways, principals enter the public sphere of educational policy.

Jenlink (2005) found that leaders "as public intellectuals are concerned with making education political, that is, making public issues of social justice and equity as part of the educational agenda, working to foster more democratic social practices that transform the space of schools" through an understanding that "Schools are sites where the intellectual activity taking place in them is inextricably linked to broader social and cultural concerns; that transforming schools is linked to transforming society" (p. 9).

As servants to students, society, and the educational system itself, principals seek to humanize processes for the sake of care, democracy, learning, and social justice. Fullan (2008) wrote, "One might say that the government level is too removed from the world of the principal, but this need not, and should not, be the case" because the ability to influence the larger system "is not a pipe dream" (pp. 48–49). Many times, in fact, policy leaders actually appreciate hearing the voices from the field. Not only is influencing the larger systems possible, but it is the responsibility of the principal as servant-leader.

Public Relations

In general, when many principals consider public relations, immediate opposing thoughts of an *us* (the school) and a *them* (the public) come to mind. The goal of a successful public-relations approach, for the servant-leader, requires moving beyond this polarizing attitude. In an effort to make this a reality, principals must consider the meaning of both *public* and *relations* as they marry to form *public relations*.

The *public*, regardless of previous experiences, cannot be and is not the enemy. Furthermore, the public is not a necessary evil. In fact, with a thorough understanding of its role and contributive ability, the public is a necessary asset. Principals must consider our public as part of the stakeholder group with a vested interest in the matters of the school. The *public* of the school principal includes parents (who expect a great education for their children), the community (who expect value from their tax-dollar investment), and the business industry (who expect competent future workers).

In essence, members of the public are the clients of the principal, and a quality education is the product they expect. It is the responsibility of a democratic public to demand transparency, expect results, and provide support to American schools. When principals truly consider members of the public as clientele and not barriers, a more appropriate understanding and appreciation is developed that is useful for all stakeholders. And, as globalization naturally occurs, the public will continue to become more demanding of results from our schools. With this in mind, the principal recognizes the public as a grouping to be served well, not feared.

A renewed examination is also required of the meaning and merits of *relations* in the term *public relations*. American principals too often view *relations* as how they deal with the public. This approach of *dealing with the public* is antithetical to the work of the servant-leader, who realizes *relations* is root for the word *relationships*. There must be capitalization of the power provided by authentic relationships with anyone, including the public, as the client of the school principal.

The strength of the principalship is woven from a web of intentional and purposeful interconnectivity with others. Hindman, Seiders, and Grant (2009) wrote that "Effective leaders know that more can be accomplished through productive relationships" and "Having the ability to establish and grow positive relationships is a necessary facet of being a good leader" (p. 1).

Success, to some degree, hinges on the principal's ability to create and maintain relationships with the public. A relationship with others holds us accountable and sets a tone of expectation for both parties. Having an authentic, service-minded relationship with someone shows a genuine care for knowing and understanding them with an ethic to support their endeavors toward personal completeness or wholeness.

With a revamped grasp of public relations, a principal has a greater opportunity for success in that particular area of leadership. According to Williamson and Blackburn (2009), "Public relations is one of the most important roles of a school leader" because "It is an effective way to create a positive image of the school and to share the school's successes" (p. 72). Furthermore, when the relationship is situated within achieving the collective vision, it has greater meaning.

Without a doubt, the public will have an impression of both the school and the principal. It is important, however, that this image be a positive one. There must be an overt attempt at gaining the public's participation in the school process. When principals involve the public, where fitting and appropriate, relationships are bolstered and productivity for stakeholders increases. With proactive approaches, the principal sets the frame for the participation. Without proactive measures such as conversations, newsletters, and other forms of communication, a negative impression is formed, and the principal is forced to be reactive.

Being faithful in the relationship with the public is critical for authenticity. Once a relationship is developed, the public expects a benefit and focused continuation of the partnership. Moreover, an open-minded principal seeks and accepts feedback from the public.

Brower and Balch (2005) found that "Stakeholder respect is critical" and "Leaders can facilitate this by being visible, asking meaningful questions of stakeholders, listening empathetically, gathering information from all levels through effective one-way and two-way communication means, and creating capacities that encourage positive and meaningful feedback about the institution" (p. 70). Principals as servant-leaders use their expertise to guide the school; however, they depend on aligning school practices, as much as possible when appropriate, with the desires of the public.

The benefits from solid public relationships are very significant for all stakeholders. Principals as servant-leaders accept their role as employees of, and for, the public. In the discharge of their duties, principals must willingly embrace the goal of shaping the school in a manner that maximizes the advantages of authentic relationships.

Legal Considerations

School principals enter their roles with years of experiences that have shaped their personal ideology. Without guidelines or rules, personal ideologies would infringe upon the rights of others. The ancient philosopher Aristotle said, "Law is reason, free from passion." There are legal considerations for every act of the principal. Rules include a combination of federal, state, and local policies of which the principal must be aware.

The principal as servant-leader accepts the authority of the governing bodies and works within the current law. When necessary, however, the leader politically advocates for laws, rules, and policies to be changed in the best interests of stakeholders. A respect for the law and a willingness to understand law is important for the school leader. Ubben, Hughes, and Norris (2007) wrote, "No one expects a principal to be a legal authority but a consciousness of the laws under which the schools operate is an essential responsibility" as "There are many situations in which principals as well as teachers engage that have legal implications" (p. 336).

At the federal level, initially, education was not specifically mentioned in either the Constitution or Bill of Rights. Because of this, education became a responsibility of the states through the tenth amendment, which basically states that powers not delegated through the Constitution are reserved for the states. However, over time, the federal government has become increasingly involved in the educational system through rules tied to funding, Supreme Court decisions, and connections of stakeholders to the amendments of the Bill of Rights.

America's founding fathers had a worthy rationale for not including education in the Constitution or Bill of Rights. They believed, by reserving education as a right of the states, schooling would remain local to students and families served. Even today, with growing federal influence, the state maintains authority to develop and implement educational systems. These systems, however, simply cannot supersede the restrictions of the federal government.

Although individual states provide the general framework for the educational system, local districts tailor systems specific to their needs and resources. At the local level, community members are elected to serve as members of the governing body, the school board. These men and women are responsible for ensuring that appropriate policies and practices are in place to provide an education to students. In their service, the board selects a superintendent of schools to execute the daily operations of the system, based upon the legal considerations of the federal, state, and local decisions.

As a responsibility, the superintendent enforces the laws and guides the board through recommendations for educational practices within the district. The superintendent selects principals and expects them to hold an awareness of the law. Ubben, Hughes, and Norris (2007) found "It is at the school building level that the policies of the local school board and the laws of the land that govern education are most often implemented," and "It is also at the school building level that most of the litigation involving the schools begins."

School principals must be cognizant of the law and how to navigate within the law to carry forward the vision of the organization. As lifelong learners, principals should stay abreast of legal considerations through readings, attendance at law conferences, and through consultation with district personnel.

As a rule, every principal should have a reference book for school law in their professional library with the ability to quickly access it as needs arise. Principals cannot become fearful of the law, stifling their practices. Instead, they should be knowledgeable and move forward with confidence in their ability to work within the legal system. Furthermore, principals should appreciate their ability to shift policy as advocates for stakeholders through appropriate governmental channels.

Positional Evolution

Another role of the principal within the context of leadership is positional evolution. In short, positional evolution means the improvement of the profession of the principalship. This idea of giving back includes anything that advances the profession, improves the profession, or solid-ifies the future of the profession.

This can be accomplished, holistically, by maturing into an effective principal as servant-leader. Beyond that, the principal completes tasks such as maintaining active membership in professional organizations, building partnerships with universities, serving on relevant panels or committees, mentoring new administrators, and seeking other creative and explicit ways to promote the principalship today and tomorrow.

Part 2

Principal Examples

In an effort to draw connections between real principals and the information provided in earlier chapters, the following three chapters were constructed. Using an acceptable formula, three principals were selected based on the outstanding successes in the area of student academic performance at their schools. To provide universal acceptability, the schools utilized were all public schools with a PK-through-twelfth-grade configuration, servicing students from ages three to nineteen.

The author as researcher interviewed the principals using Laub's (1999) model, which defines servant-leadership as "an understanding and practice of leadership that places the good of those led over the self-interest of the leader" (p. 81). The model's components consider whether leaders value individuals, develop people, build community, practice authenticity, provide leadership, and share power. *qualities of a great principal*

To provide a natural flow in the interviews, the principals were asked a set of questions and responded both from a philosophical and practical application standpoint. The narratives of these successful principals are insightful and highlight servant-leadership in action with the recognition that each principal was stronger in certain areas of leadership while weaker in other areas. The names of the schools as well as the individuals involved are all pseudonyms.

The goal of the reader is to make connections between the servant-leadership of these principals and the ISLLC standards of vision, instruction, organization, collaboration, ethics, and politics. Readers seeking to gain appreciation of the standards application will benefit from attempting to extract the standards from the narratives as well as seeking to discover interplay between the six standards in the stories of these professional, and successful, school principals.

NINE

Mrs. Miller at Cypress School

INTRODUCTION

As I turned into the pasture-like campus of Cypress School, I noticed a collection of brick buildings with green metal roofs. Unable to identify the campus administration building, I searched for assistance and noticed someone, presumably the school's janitor, riding a lawn mower at a high rate of speed. As he noticed this bamboozled driver making circles in the school's parking lot, he slammed on his brakes and his mower came to an abrupt halt. He motioned for me, with a wave of his hand, to drive in his direction.

As I pulled up and rolled down my window, he cut off his engine. I asked, "Will you tell me where the principal's office is located?" He pointed to a covered opening between two buildings and said, "Right through there." I thanked him and continued driving until I noticed two parked cars. I said to myself, "This must be the place."

As I opened my vehicle door, I was inundated with the overwhelming smell of freshly cut grass. Recognizing that some campuses mature with grass and weeds during the summer, I was impressed with the well-manicured grounds of Cypress School. I walked toward the nearest door and stepped inside to find the longest hallway I had ever seen in a school. Honestly, I wanted to shout "hello," to see if the word would reproduce itself with a repeating "hello" like I have heard on television.

The walls were a pure, wholesome white, and the fluorescent lights radiated a dazzling brightness. As a school administrator, amazed with these findings, I stopped walking, placed my briefcase on the tile floor, and simply gazed at the cleanliness of the building. The floor and walls were impeccable and I was certain this was a new facility, only later to discover the building was built in the mid-1950s. Yes, the cleanest school

I had ever seen was built nearly sixty years ago. I recognized an office and advanced toward it, excited to share my findings with the school's principal as if she was not aware of her spotless facility.

As I entered the office, I was greeted by a teenage girl who was sitting in the "secretary chair." In her north-central Louisianan drawl, the girl said, "Hi there! Can I help you?" Stirred by her spunkiness, I responded, "Why yes, you may. I'm looking for Principal Miller." She said, "She is on the phone right now, but you can wait for her." Concerned that the weight of my briefcase was too burdensome, she offered, "Would you like to set your bag up here on the counter? Or, you can just have a seat." Before I could respond to her proposal, Mrs. Miller walked out from her office and said, "I'm glad to see you." I said, "Likewise" and she presented her hand for a firm handshake before telling me to "Come on in."

As I turned the corner and entered the principal's office, I was taken aback by the room's magnificent illumination. Also, I was intrigued by the furniture arrangement of her office. Instead of a large and ornate "I am the principal" desk, she had a tiny built-in that was off-centered in the room, coupled with a small, plastic rolling chair. Additionally, instead of flamboyant cabinetry, she had a local carpenter create built-ins, using native lumber. The office had a bright openness that, for me, removed asymmetrical power relations and created an open, collaborative environment.

I said, "This is an interesting office." With a smile, she questioned, "How so?" Still, I was in awe, but responded "It's not oppressive to others." With even a bigger smile, she voiced, "I like people to be comfortable in this office. There used to be one of those big mahogany desks in here and I had it removed. I think this is a better fit for us." Then, I asked her if she was ready to begin the interview process and she said, "Sure, but let me get you a Coke first." Realizing that in the South a "Coke" could be any number of flavored drinks, I simply said, "Oh, no thank you. I brought my water." Then, we began.

MRS. MILLER

Mrs. Miller was a soft-spoken and eloquent principal in her early sixties. Despite her self-proclaimed "grandmotherly" persona, at one point during our interview, I was erroneously convinced she had military experience under her belt. Her responses to interview prompts were effectively calculated, developed, and articulated. Mrs. Miller was an excellent verbal communicator.

She called Cypress her home, indicating that she had lived there for most of her life. She received her bachelors of science in 1965 and her masters of education in 1970. She even added the "plus 30 graduate hours" past her master's, even though she indicated that it was "actually more like fifty." By trade, she taught middle-school English for thirty-one years; then, accepted the principalship at Cypress School. Mrs. Miller made the transition from teacher at Cypress School directly into the principalship.

She said,

> I was on this faculty for a number of years as a teacher and I have thoughts about being promoted from within. I think there is a positive side and a downside as well [to being internally promoted]. Initially, I don't know that my faculty saw me as being worthy, or up to the task. The pervading thought here was that high-school teachers have cornered the market on school administration. A common thought is that elementary and junior-high teachers need to stay in their classrooms and let secondary teachers advance to positions that require all the thinking. I think that they have come to see me as consistent, fair, available, on duty, on the campus. As a matter of fact, teachers complain frequently that "you're never in your office." To me, I perceive this as a compliment.

When asked why she selected the teaching and educational leadership profession, Mrs. Miller said,

> Approximately ten years ago, there were initiatives statewide to recruit and develop school leaders. Various programs in school leadership were available in the local universities. Because I'm the perpetual learner and needed a new challenge, I participated in and completed two of those programs. I love learning and I've been involved in school since I was four years old. I suppose I have lived and breathed school, the activities of school, and learning for as long as I can recall. I taught in the junior high for years, and I really believed that I could make a difference. I had a working knowledge of boys and girls and learning. I felt that I knew curriculum, pedagogy, teachers, and students. I had firm notions of what a school should look like and how it should function. And, I had the desire to lead a school. I know that I have the heart and the vision to improve my school.

Mrs. Miller was selected for this study because Cypress School has achieved a high level of sustained school improvement growth. During the immediate three years, Cypress School had made approximately a 26-percent increase in student learning according to accountability measures. Cypress has received numerous awards for academic excellence over the past few years. Interestingly, however, even with the mounting emphasis on standardized tests or school performance, Mrs. Miller never spoke directly of accountability movements, with the exception of mentioning that Cypress School had "taken a dive" the year before she became principal.

Instead of considering a principal's or school's success based on accountability scores, Mrs. Miller described a successful principal as "the leader of a healthy school [where] boys and girls are leaning and teachers

have a professional attitude that <u>learning is serious business</u>." Furthermore, she described herself as a principal by stating, "I am dedicated to
students and their well-being and to teachers and staff providing services
to children. I'm consistently available to children and adults, a facilitator
and encourager, and am determined to help my school to continue its
academic growth."

DECONSTRUCTION THROUGH LAUB'S SERVANT-LEADERSHIP ORGANIZATIONAL MODEL

Following an analysis and coding of Mrs. Miller's stories, I found all six
attributes of Laub's servant-leadership organizational model's characteristics evident in her belief system and practices as a principal. Some of
these characteristics were more profound than others. To follow, each of
Laub's six servant-leadership organizational model's characteristics will
be exemplified in the beliefs and practices of Mrs. Miller through her
personal story. These stories, turned into narrative, form a truth and
reality for this principal.

Servant-Leaders Value People

Valuing people means trusting and believing in people, serving others' needs before his or her own, and <u>utilizing receptive, nonjudgmental
listening</u>. The following narrative details Mrs. Miller's beliefs and experiences with this characteristic.

When Mrs. Miller was questioned about the value of individuals at
Cypress School, she rolled her eyes and voiced a small grunt, interpreted
by this researcher to mean, "Where would I be without the people of
Cypress School?" After about a ten-second pause, Mrs. Miller said, "People are invaluable. Absolutely invaluable!" Then, she supplied me with a
firm stare for what seemed like an eternity.

Basically, she wanted me to know and fully understand her stance on
this matter. Then, as the silent awkwardness resonated in her office, she
continued, finally, by saying, "The heart of school, in my thinking, is not
the building or the grounds—it's the humans. I work to make sure all
people on this campus understand the value of their contribution to the
smooth operation of Cypress School."

Mrs. Miller shared two instances of her value for her teachers in their
time of great illness. One instance required her to affirm her support of a
teacher by recommending his continued employment despite his termi-
nal illness, while another required her to personally assume the teaching
duties of an ill teacher. She said,

> Two years ago, one of the more controversial members of my faculty, a
> veteran teacher, was diagnosed with terminal cancer. A vocal segment

of the community called for his resignation. The teacher asked to continue teaching as long as his health permitted, vowing that he would certainly not harm the learning of children. A considerable furor ensued. As the principal, I was the individual on the spot to recommend continued employment or termination. The superintendent indicated that he would support whatever decision I made. I believed that [ill] teacher, who had devoted thirty years to young people and school, would conduct himself honorably and step aside when he could no longer perform his duties. I knew my response to this situation would send a strong message to my faculty and community. So, I recommended continued employment. The decision was not universally popular, but it did communicate my steadfast and strong support for and belief in my faculty. The sense of community on our campus strengthened enormously. Virtually every other member of the faculty said to me, "You did the right thing." The superintendent accepted my recommendation and advised the board to continue employment for this teacher. My beleaguered teacher returned to his duties, has served admirably despite physical challenges, and has been a sterling example of courage and tenacity for his colleagues and for his students. I believe daily engagement in meaningful activity, such as coming to school and working every day, has been a major factor in this teacher's survival. He is in his third year of remission [and is still teaching at Cypress School].

When another classroom teacher became critically ill for an extended period of time,

> I assumed the planning and many of the teaching tasks performed by that teacher. Daily, I worked with students, addressing their academic and emotional needs. The experience deepened my belief that being an effective classroom teacher requires tremendous energy, sharp focus, and genuine concern for all aspects of students' lives. I believe the faculty perceived that experience positively and understand the high regard I have for each classroom and teacher on this campus.

Servant-Leaders Develop People

Developing people means providing opportunities for learning and growth, modeling appropriate behavior, and building others up through encouragement and affirmation.

Mrs. Miller indicated that her greatest disappointment as a principal has been the lack of professional development opportunities at Cypress School. She said, "We haven't had the professional development that I perceive we need. In one area, I see that as a district problem because I'm not allowed the time or financial resources." In touring the school, Mrs. Miller began walking toward the door of a portable building and I asked, "Are you full beyond your facility's capacity?" She said, "No. This is a computer lab the district established for professional development. We've only been in here for a handful of meetings since they established it." Inside the cooled building, there must have been thirty fully functioning computers and flat-screen monitors available for use. Additionally, there was technology mounted on the wall and projection equipment hanging from the ceiling. I sensed a disappointment in her district leadership for not offering more parish-wide professional development opportunities.

Furthermore, Mrs. Miller discussed her dissatisfaction with some of her teachers not seeking higher degrees. She said,

> I have several teachers here who've earned their bachelor's degree and, I'm ashamed to say, they have not gone beyond their bachelor's. They've taught for several years and there is no inclination that they'll work toward anything else. That's an irritant that I cannot express. It's completely beyond me how a person could be in a classroom year after year and not want to continue to learn [through additional formal training].

Concerning in-house professional development, Mrs. Miller stated, "I encourage my teachers to participate in trainings. I believe, in education, that developing people is crucial. Several times a week, I use the phrase 'we're life-long learners.' When we're stagnant, we decay."

Overall, I detected disgust from Mrs. Miller when she reflected upon her work in developing people. I didn't perceive disgust stemming from a lack of her personal effort, but instead, there was repugnance at her current inability to motivate the entire faculty toward voluntarily seeking professional growth. For example, she spoke of her failures with peer observations. "At one point, we observed one another. The culture of the school didn't allow that to work. Maybe it was before its time." Later, when discussing barriers to leadership, she shared,

> There have been several barriers to my leadership. One has been with the faculty that did not share some of my vision. I believe I learned that there are going to be some folks who never come on board. I'm idealistic enough to believe that they all should. Some faculty members, those same ones who don't do professional development, are barriers. Professional development at the central-office level has been a barrier. Teachers need opportunities, incentives, and strong encouragement. I frankly believe it ought to be mandatory for teachers and administrators to show professional growth.

Servant-Leaders Build Community

Building community means building strong personal relationships, working collaboratively with others, and valuing the differences of others. The following narrative details Mrs. Miller's beliefs and experiences with this characteristic.

During our time together, Mrs. Miller referred to her school, several times, as a *learning community.* For example, she said, "It's important to our school that every segment of our learning community feels involved and valued." She spoke of togetherness, collaboration, and relationships at various instances during the interview. While on a vacation in the Northeast, she saw a school's sign that made a lasting impression, which resonated and then came to personal fruition once she became the Cypress School principal. With the memory of that sign, she purchased several large signs for Cypress School, "stealing the idea," which proclaimed "This is Cypress" and posted them at various campus entrances. Moreover, she often takes a "This is Cypress" stance when dealing with inappropriate student behavior. "Once, there was a little boy who had done something he shouldn't have done. I asked him, 'Where are you?' He answered 'Cypress.' I told him, 'That's right. This is Cypress and we don't act like that at Cypress.'"

Mrs. Miller provides opportunities for her student body, of all ages, to spend time together.

> It's not uncommon for folks here to mingle, especially the youngsters. For the most part, we do come together. We want our pre-K through twelve activities to be together, even though we're miles apart in interests because of grade levels. We come together, we cross lines, and we do things together. We're a community and that entails everything that it is. There are folks in the community who are cooperative and pleasant. There are a few that are difficult. There are some I'd like to exile. I believe we work together as a living, breathing, moving organism.

Mrs. Miller explained that her relationships with students are very important.

> My door is typically open and, on any given day, children from fairly young to the high-school senior will walk into my office and say, "Mrs. Miller, I need to talk to you now." I don't perceive that to be disrespectful; but instead, I see it as an honorable thing. They see me as someone they can talk to. There is openness between us; but they also see me as fairly stern. Students also see me as a grandmother-type who is somehow connected because I taught their brothers, sisters, mamas, or daddies. I want students to feel connected, important, and nurtured. I make an effort to know each student's name. When I greet students, I deliberately say their names and initiate some pleasant conversation. I believe the students' perceptions are, "Mrs. Miller knows me, and she likes me."

Also, she spoke of developing and sustaining relationships with the community outside the school's walls and provided examples of those initiatives.

> I want them supporting their children, grandchildren, nieces, and nephews. For example, we had a year-end program for our pre-K kids and the auditorium was full. I thought, "Where did these people come from?" During the day, we can have a musical and the auditorium is

full. I jokingly think "Don't these people have a job?" But that's support.

Schools are often faced with the tragic deaths of students. Cypress School, under the direction of Mrs. Miller, also experienced a loss. The incident killed one student and left another with a lifelong injury. She said,

> On our part of the planet, hunting, fishing, and fast pick-up trucks are the heart of virtually every young male's world. Winding country roads invite speed and daredevil deeds. In the fall of 2003, one member of our student body sacrificed his sixteen year-old life "just havin' fun playin' chick'n" in a pick-up hurtling toward another vehicle [which was] driven by a friend. In the incident, another student sustained massive brain injuries that forever changed his life. He will never function as an independent adult. Our school community was unified in its unconditional support for the affected families in the days immediately following the accident and long after. Because our school community is small, practically every high-school student and teacher was well acquainted with the two youngsters and their families. At school, teachers served as counselors, primarily listening and providing framework for students to process the tragedy. Without heavy-handedness, moralizing, or sermons, I do believe our students absorbed many valuable truths about the fragile nature of life and the consequences of unwise decisions. When the student with massive brain injury was able to return to school, the entire school, students, faculty, [and] staff looked after "J" and all his needs. He was perpetually "lost," but there was always someone to guide [or] accompany him to his next class or activity. "J" was able to graduate with his peers. At that graduation ceremony, a single white rose lay in the chair that would have been occupied by our dear friend.

Moving on, Mrs. Miller shared a story about securing community involvement and building relationships.

> Our teachers and students organize and develop a health fair every fall. To maximize participation and positive effect, I suggested that the fair be scheduled to coincide with our Grandparents' Day. Virtually every segment of our learning community is engaged. While at school, these adults are invited to visit classrooms and encouraged to volunteer. Evaluations and outcomes of this activity are positive.

Touring her facility, Mrs. Miller introduced me to her school's auditorium. I asked, "Now what is this used for?" After giving me a host of school-related uses, she said, "I encourage the community to use it too for their events. I figure if it's here in the community, we should all benefit from it. So, I don't have a problem with it being used."

Finally, she spoke about her working relationships with her faculty and staff. Mrs. Miller said school leadership is "being able and willing to collaborate with colleagues in planning, developing, and executing procedures that will result in a pleasant learning environment, teaching environment, effective instruction, and genuine learning. In my opinion, the principal must be an integral part, a working part of the team that addresses and works through challenges." This view of leadership extends to her relationship with her custodial staff.

> I have a lady janitor who surveys the campus and writes me lists [of things that need to be addressed or completed]. We have such a relationship that she fusses at me if I pick up something. I'm not beyond working and picking things up. She takes that as a shot at her. I have very intelligent people working in custodial positions. They basically tell me "You do the principaling and we'll do the janitorial work" and that's basically what happens.

Servant-Leaders Display Authenticity

Displaying authenticity means being open and accountable to others, having a willingness to learn from others, and maintaining integrity and trust. The following narrative details Mrs. Miller's beliefs and experiences with this characteristic.

When questioned about her beliefs regarding authenticity in leadership, Mrs. Miller responded,

> It's a daily affair and I don't know that I can give you a specific example. I think I'm authentic every day in my perception. I think the way that I deal with people on a daily basis shows that I'm positive and nurturing. I can also be very pragmatic. I think that if there is no authenticity, there will be enormous difficulties.

Later, she continued,

> My notion of leadership is as one who is an integral part of a team, as a facilitator, as an encourager, as a cheerleader, as somebody who is gently pushing and constantly uplifting others. If that's not real, I'm confident that school will unravel. What I believe and value Monday through Friday at school is synonymous with my beliefs off the campus.

Mrs. Miller believes principals should enjoy the work of, and have credibility in, teaching.

> I've always been genuinely in love with the classroom. I value what teachers do in the classroom. I've been there. I know what should go on. I have very, very firm ideas of what should go on and I value what they do every day. I believe a leader needs to have worn the cloak of a teacher. I'm not saying a leader has to be in the classroom for thirty years, but I'm saying you have to have known the victories and defeats of the classroom.

Servant-Leaders Provide Leadership

Providing leadership means envisioning the future, taking initiative, and clarifying goals. The following narrative details Mrs. Miller's beliefs and experiences with this characteristic.

Mrs. Miller is cognizant of the formal role she plays as the educational leader of Cypress. She said,

> I believe there needs to be a person who is ultimately in charge because of the hierarchy of our culture's operation. Leaders must be the voice or spokesperson. That needs to be recognized. Here, the buck stops with Mrs. Miller. I can revel in successes and victories, but I'm also responsible for when things don't go right. There needs to be that person that handles situations when they arise. I believe the successful school leader constantly communicates positives about students, teachers, and the school. The leader expresses high expectations for the entire learning community, understands teaching and learning, participates actively in planning and in improving learning, guards teaching and learning, collaborates with colleagues, shares leadership, recognizes achievement, honors the culture of the school, and maintains a sense of humor.

[handwritten margin note: Positives, positives, positives]

During our interview, Mrs. Miller only directly mentioned standardized test scores and accountability ratings one time. This lone accountability mention included an explanation of her perception that Cypress School needed to make changes in order to improve academically.

> I came aboard after a year of laxness at this school. Our scores took a dive. The dive was attributed to a lack of leadership. When our abysmal scores were shared with faculty, we grieved together. Then, my response was, "Folks, we've had a bad run, but things must change. I want us to dig in. We can sit around and whine, moan, and groan; but the only way for us to start climbing the ladder is to dig in, look at the test scores, analyze our weak areas, and forge a workable plan just for us. We can't do anything about history, but learn from it." After studying our test results closely, the faculty and I determined that each teacher had to focus instruction to match what was being required by state assessments. Working harder and smarter is critical to ongoing success. The leadership thing had to do with us being in a slump and I said, "Folks, we either stay here or move out. And, if I'm going to be in that office, I don't want to be in that slump. I know how to get us out and we've got to suck it up and get to working hard." With boys and girls, learning is work.

[handwritten margin note: ?]

[handwritten margin note: Teaching to the test]

Servant-Leaders Share Leadership

Sharing leadership means facilitating a shared vision, sharing power and releasing control, and sharing status and promoting others. The following narrative details Mrs. Miller's beliefs and experiences with this characteristic.

Mrs. Miller referred to herself as the "consummate sharer" during the interview. In regards to sharing leadership, she noted, "I have such good people around me. To the outsider, it might be difficult to identify the principal of this school." Her first story about sharing leadership related to her assistant principal.

> Cypress did not have an active assistant principal when I became principal. I worked hard to acquire the services of such an individual. When Mrs. G expressed an interest in school leadership, I encouraged her to complete the certification process. She did. Mrs. G now teaches three hours and performs assistant principal duties the remaining four hours. During the past four years, Mrs. G has focused on fine-tuning discipline issues, but she also leads faculty meetings, study groups, and supervises student activities.

Then, she spoke of assigning responsibilities to different faculty members.

> On this campus, different activities belong to different people. Mrs. So-and-so does the pageant. As long as Mrs. So-and-so does it, is living and breathing, I let her do it. Visitors often don't know who the principal is here at Cypress. I don't run around the campus on stilts or with a principal badge. This may sound corporate. I believe if principals surround themselves with good, quality people and provide fertile ground for their growth, they will make good things happen. I feel strongly that folks are most likely to perform at their peak when they are empowered to make decisions that directly affect themselves, ownership. For example, the three custodians here develop their schedules based on the routines of their assigned buildings. They are self-directed, take enormous pride in their work, and are extremely territorial and loyal to their buildings. The custodians are all about the campus and in each building and space every day. They constantly evaluate situations and solve custodial dilemmas. They keep me informed and offer suggestions. Bus drivers and food technicians on this campus also exhibit territorial loyalties. They are consistently required to have a voice in the issues that affect them. Teachers develop and own their programs. Within the established framework, they are afforded the license and encouraged to practice their teaching craft as creatively as they choose.

CONCLUSIONS

Mrs. Miller is a practicing servant-leader school principal. While she never indicated she was a servant-leader, she certainly embodies Laub's servant-leadership organizational model's characteristics. The servant-leadership characteristics most prevalent in Mrs. Miller, reflected in on our time together, were valuing people, building community, displaying authenticity, providing leadership, and sharing leadership. These five characteristics form the primary basis for her leadership; however, the characteristic of developing people was noted as an area that needed additional development, based on the requirements of Laub's servant-leadership model. Furthermore, Mrs. Miller was deeply passionate about her position. She indicated, "I dearly love what I do. It's gratifying when I see boys and girls learning, when I see teachers at the height of their art. But I also have a sense that it can always be better. I see myself as, in some respect, somebody wanting a challenge. I can never get comfortable. You'll start sliding backwards, or catching dust, or getting into the slug category." From a quantitative standpoint, Cypress School, under the leadership of Mrs. Miller, has made tremendous school performance gains since she has become the school's principal.

Needing to get back "on the road" following our session together, I began creeping toward the door. However, with each step toward ending our interview, Mrs. Miller had one more thing to add, one more snippet of a story to tell. From my perspective, she was devoted to and excited about her school and could have talked about her students, faculty, campus, and experiences for an extended period of time. Then, as I was almost out the door, she asked, "What good things are you guys doing at your school?" After I shared a few of my favorite initiatives, she continued with one last question. She asked, "What do you think about Cypress?" I told her, "I think Cypress School is lucky to have you as their principal." With the exterior door half open and one foot outside, I added, "Oh yeah, tell your janitors 'good job.' This is the cleanest school I've ever seen." Then, on my way to my vehicle, I stepped on chewed bubble gum and thought to myself, "Wow. They even have this problem in Cypress School."

TEN

Mr. Smith at Pine School

INTRODUCTION

When I entered the seemingly empty administration building at Pine School on a humid June morning, I immediately noticed a simple patriotic décor hanging from the lobby wall. These furnishings were not a bold statement of a red, white, and blue America, but instead, were a simple, and almost hidden, assertion of the school's underlying Americanism. Within a few moments, a middle-aged female secretary hurried from a back room into the reception area to attend to my presence.

Since I wasn't a Pine School stakeholder, she asked, with an innate and puzzled curiosity, "Can I help you, sir?" I shared that I had a nine o'clock a.m. appointment with Mr. Smith, the principal, and would wait for him to become available. The secretary leaned into Mr. Smith's office and said, "There's somebody here for you." From inside his office, Mr. Smith yelled to me, "I'll be right with you Chief, hold on." To better understand what was taking place, the secretary walked over to me, now unafraid of my presence, and said, "Sorry I didn't see you when you first came in. I was in the back cutting my cantaloupe." She smiled and continued, "Do you want some of my cantaloupe?" I politely refused by stating, "No, but that was kind of you to ask."

Momentarily, Mr. Smith darted from his office, and said, "Good morning, Chief. I guess you're here for the interview." I said, "Yes, it is a pleasure to be here." As Mr. Smith led me toward his office, I noticed he was wearing a t-shirt, mesh shorts, and tennis shoes. Mr. Smith, clearly, was comfortable on his campus during the summer break. As we walked into his office, he pushed a rolling garbage can out of the doorway and said, "Excuse the mess, Chief. I'm trying to remodel." As I began to set up, Mr. Smith said, "I've got to run to the gym and check on some work-ers. I'll be back in a few minutes."

Once I was situated, I took advantage of his absence and began ana-lyzing the interior decorations of his office, looking into Mr. Smith's hid-den curriculum. He had his school's mission statement posted along with his diplomas, a few family pictures, a mounted largemouth bass, an em-broidered Bible verse, and a framed poster hanging behind his chair that proclaimed, "God Bless America." There was an unspoken loyalty be-tween God and country in this administrative office, even if not overt. The displayed Bible verse was Matthew 6:33, which read "But seek ye first the kingdom of God, and his righteousness; and all these things shall be added unto you." After a few moments, the former coach-turned-principal darted back into the office and said, "Chief, how 'bout some coffee?" I, after being offered cantaloupe from the secretary and coffee from the principal, realized they were a hospitable crew. I had yet to determine, however, why I had earned the designation of "Chief."

MR. SMITH

Mr. Smith, a forty-one-year-old white male, is an eighteen-year veteran of the education profession. He earned his bachelor of science degree in 1988 and immediately began teaching social studies and physical educa-tion at Pine School. He completed his master of education in administra-tion and moved into an assistant principalship. After serving as an assist-ant principal for three years, Mr. Smith accepted the principal's position at Pine School. Mr. Smith lives in the community and his entire educa-tional career has been at Pine. The totality of his educational career has been spent, voluntarily, at Pine School. When asked why he selected the teaching and educational leadership profession, Mr. Smith said,

> Well, you know. We all get into education because we enjoy working with kids. We like seeing student success. I enjoyed working as a class-room teacher, but I felt this principalship was something I could do and was capable of doing. In all honesty, it is a stepping stone to a supervis-or position, which is one of my career goals. I want to be a supervisor at the central office, if not become a superintendent. I feel like quality central-office personnel know what it's like to be in the trenches at a school. If I ever become a supervisor, I want to know what it's like to wear the shoes of a principal, to know what it's like to be in the trenches every day. The principalship is a stepping stone to a career goal.

Mr. Smith was selected for this study because Pine School has achieved a high level of sustained school improvement growth. During the past three years, Pine School has grown approximately 25 percent in account-ability measures. The school has been showered with awards.

When questioned about this accountability success, Mr. Smith spi-raled his way, humbly, as he stated,

> A successful principal is one who provides an atmosphere for students and employees to come to school each day and feel safe. The environ-ment must be conducive to learning. It's an atmosphere you foster with students, faculty, and staff. We're all here for one reason. As a princi-pal, it doesn't take rocket science, but policies must be in place. If you get too particular about small things, you're chasing the wrong rabbit. You must be realistic and provide a caring atmosphere. I fully expect that our test scores will fall at some point. Those kinds of things hap-pen. I'm not so dumb to think we're going to grow every year. I don't think test scores are the total of a school. I don't think we should gauge the success of a school, or an individual, based on a test score. There should be other variables [considered when evaluating the quality of a school].

While he may believe other factors are important in evaluating schools, according to Pine School's accountability score, it is a success.

DECONSTRUCTION THROUGH LAUB'S SERVANT-LEADERSHIP ORGANIZATIONAL MODEL

Following an analysis and coding of Mr. Smith's stories, I found attrib-utes of all six of Laub's servant-leadership organizational model's charac-teristics evident in his belief system and practices as a principal. To fol-low, each of Laub's six servant-leadership organizational model's charac-teristics will be exemplified through the beliefs and practices of Mr. Smith. These stories, turned into narrative, form a truth and reality for this principal.

Servant-Leaders Value People

Valuing people means trusting and believing in people, serving oth-ers' needs before his or her own, and by receptive, nonjudgmental listen-ing. The following narrative details Mr. Smith's beliefs and experiences with this characteristic.

During our interview, Mr. Smith was adamant in his belief in the value of people and their held potential to creatively do their assigned jobs and, collectively, improve Pine School. Mr. Smith trusts and believes in the personnel of Pine School and serves their needs before attending to his own.

Referring to his value of quality personnel, Mr. Smith said,

If you didn't have people, you wouldn't have school to begin with. You've got to have students. You've got to have teachers. I think quality people make things work in a school setting. The people make the difference. I try to put quality people in places. When I replace somebody, I try to make sure and replace that person with someone at least as good, if not better, than the person who left. It doesn't just mean classroom teachers. You have to have a custodian who really cares about what they do at school. If the classrooms or gym aren't clean, you're setting up an environment that's not conducive to learning. Even a cafeteria worker [is important to the quality of a school]. Those ladies down there try to provide the best meals they can every day for our kids with what they have to work with and that's the kind of people you want. I don't think it's just people, but quality people. When it comes to students and parents, we take what we're given and work with that. But when it comes to staffing, it's quality people that help make the difference.

When speaking of valuing people's ability to perform as professionals, he indicated to me that he is not a micromanager and at seven different times during the interview reiterated this. For example, he said,

I don't micromanage. If I'm going to micromanage, I might as well do everything by myself. I don't go tell my good math teacher how to teach math. I don't go tell my science teacher how to teach science. I'm not going to do it. That's not in my bag of tricks. I put people in places because they're professionals and know what needs to be done in the classrooms. As long as you're putting the best possible people in the classrooms, you're doing well. I know good teaching in the classroom when I see it. Good teaching is good teaching. I make sure my teachers know they have my support and I try to provide them with the materials and things they need to produce quality students. I allow them to do the things they need to do in their classrooms and be creative. I give teachers the freedom to be creative. If we were all robots, I wouldn't need to be here. As a leader, I must allow them to do what they need to do in the classroom and support them as they do it. Whatever they need, I get it. There isn't a classroom teacher here who would tell you that I don't give them the things they need to do their job effectively. I allow people to be themselves; to be the creative persons they need to be to make sure students are getting a quality education. As long as I see good teaching and students learning, I don't micromanage. Teachers appreciate that.

Sometimes, however—although rarely, according to Mr. Smith—teachers need guidance. He said, "If I feel like a teacher just isn't getting it done, I address that. I do it in a professional manner. I don't holler and scream at teachers. We try to hit it with a positive attitude. Start positive, not negative. People appreciate that. There may be a time to go negative at something, but start positive."

Servant-Leaders Develop People

Developing people means providing opportunities for learning and growth, modeling appropriate behavior, and building up others through encouragement and affirmation. The following narrative details Mr. Smith's beliefs and experiences with this characteristic.

Probably stemming from his years as a high-school coach, Mr. Smith is cautious about the success of his school and is not satisfied with its current status. He believes Pine School can do better and believes his personnel must gain additional professional development for that continued success.

In general, Mr. Smith said,

> I believe there is always room for improvement. I provide teachers the opportunities through staff development to encourage teachers to grow professionally. I don't think you can ever say, "I know it all." If you ever get to that point, get out of the business. The profession changes. Take a good, quality teacher from twenty-five years ago and they couldn't make it in here today because it's not the same environment. I don't see it getting easier any time soon. I think all of us need to do professional development. I've been to the last two national principals' conferences. I had the opportunity to go to the elementary- or secondary-school conference and I chose the secondary conference. Also, there was a situation where a principal at another school was unable to go to an elementary conference. The superintendent called me up and said, "Your test scores are going up and I want you to go." I looked at my calendar and was able to go, so I went. It was good for me. Hopefully, I model professional growth to classroom teachers. I feel like if I model that as a principal, my teachers will do the same. I've never turned a teacher down even if it's during the middle of the week if they see a need to go to a conference or professional development. We find the funding to pay for it. I encourage them to try to grow professionally. Success is not something that you can earn and are done with. If you start getting comfortable and feeling good about yourself, the school will go south on you quick.

Mr. Smith shared a story about a young teacher that he, along with his assistant principal Mr. Long, were assisting. Evidently, this new teacher was struggling with his planning for the needs of the entire class period. Mr. Smith said,

> We've got a junior-high social-studies teacher who is still growing. His test scores went up ten points this year but there is still room for improvement. One of the big things we see with new teachers is managing time in the classroom. They plan for certain things, then realize the students are sitting there for fifteen minutes at the end of class without anything to do. The lesson is over. This teacher has this problem. We're working with that to help him maximize his time. You must teach from bell to bell. Doing that cuts down on discipline problems in the class-

room. When you can keep students on task, it's a win-win situation for everybody. We are trying to help him. He is growing. He is still struggling with maximizing instructional minutes for the hour. We've allowed this teacher to go model other classroom teachers and we've even sent him to other schools. I want to get him the help he needs to grow professionally. I hope that teachers would say that "Mr. Smith allowed me to do my job and supported me. He gave me everything I needed to do my job and supported me. He cared for me."

Servant-Leaders Build Community

Building community means building strong personal relationships, working collaboratively with others, and valuing the differences of others. The following narrative details Mr. Smith's beliefs and experiences with this characteristic.

With Mr. Smith, community was probably the most prevalent servant-leadership characteristic. While events, in his opinion, have forced community to develop at his school, he facilitated the process. To him, the school is his family and he deeply cares for each and every person there. Furthermore, in his opinion, a series of faculty and student deaths have cultivated a sense of community at Pine School.

Speaking of Pine School as a family, Mr. Smith said, "We have a family. That's what I want. There are a lot of people that work for me now that were here in some form when I first got into teaching [here at Pine School]. I know what kind of people they are. They supported me and I support them. It goes to the family atmosphere we have here. I've even got teachers who didn't know me from Adam when I hired them and they'll tell you they like the family environment here. It's not just a job." To validate his family environment, Mr. Smith informed me that he presently has applications from twelve teachers requesting employment at Pine School. However, he joked, "Of course . . . I don't have a spot for them."

Mr. Smith is very deeply concerned about caring for his students and his faculty. After the interview, for example, he told the school secretary, "Why don't you go ahead and go home for the day. I know you've got some stuff to do at home. Don't worry about the school. I'll catch the phones." When talking about his commitment to students, he said,

> My students know I care about them. First of all, they know I care about their safety. They know I care about their well-being. They know I care that they're getting a good education at school. I think my students know I have a genuine concern for their well-being and the education they're receiving at Pine. Kids have to know that you're genuinely concerned about them. If you want kids to go to the end of the Earth for you, going the extra mile, they have to know that you're genuinely concerned about them. You can't be their buddy, but you

can be their friend. If you build genuine bonds, they'll give you their best effort in the long run.

After being asked if Pine School had a strong community, Mr. Smith said, "There is an old saying that it takes a community to raise a child and I firmly believe that. I don't think one teacher can do it; it takes an entire school. I think we have a strong community here at Pine. We do; we're strong."

Additionally supporting his strong sense of community, Mr. Smith shared his experiences dealing with death while principal at Pine School. With tears forming in his eyes, a shakiness in his voice, and a slight tremble in his being, Mr. Smith shared,

> I've been at this school for seven years in administration. In that time, we've lost five kids, three teachers, and numerous other family members [to death]. I didn't want to create this community; it just happened. When those things happen to a school our size, you can't help but build community. My superintendent keeps asking "Mr. Smith, how are you making it?" I tell her we've got two choices—we can either sink or we can swim. For me, I refuse to let Pine School sink on my watch. It's not going to happen. We're going to pull it together, pick up the pieces, and move on. We're going to support each other and that's what I've got here. We're going to pick up the pieces and move forward. Our school has been set up to fail so many times and it just hasn't happened. I haven't created these conditions, but as the educational leader of the school, it has built community. We've had reasons to give up.

Mr. Smith then moved into specific examples of the deaths impacting his school and building community.

> My first year as principal, I lost a classroom teacher to cancer. We buried her the week before we came back from Christmas break. We had to deal with that. I've lost students. We lost two kids the week before Labor Day one year. We hadn't been in school but a few weeks. We buried those kids the Sunday before Labor Day. When we came back to school on Tuesday, we had a tough job. When you've got kids as well-liked as those two, quality young men, you better be ready to pick up the pieces. In that situation, it could have gone south for Pine School real quick, but we were headed in the right direction by the end of the week. This past Friday, my teacher named Daisy Crenshaw lost a husband to cancer and we buried him. There were a lot of people from Pine School at the funeral. That's what makes schools work—caring about people. My wife and I drove over to see her the other day when Mrs. Crenshaw's husband was on life-support and the family had to make a decision about what to do with his life. I wasn't there because I had to be; I was there because I wanted to be. We care about people at this school.

Servant-Leaders Display Authenticity

Displaying authenticity means being open and accountable to others, having a willingness to learn from others, and maintaining integrity and trust. The following narrative details Mr. Smith's beliefs and experiences with this characteristic.

In speaking of authenticity, Mr. Smith indicated a need for principals to be "real." He spoke of holding a congruency between espoused values and values in use. He said,

> I have to be real. I can't say one thing and do another. If I'm not going to expect it from myself, I'm not going to expect it from others. If I expect teachers to do their best, I'll be prepared to do my best each day when I step into that truck each morning. I'm not going to tell teachers one thing, and me do another. I've got to be real and on the up-and-up. I can't hide that; people aren't dumb. I've got to be honest. If I can't hold myself to high expectations, I'm not the man for the job.

Also, he indicated his cognizance of his own limitations and the importance of careful consideration of all viewpoints in decision-making. Mr. Smith shared,

> I don't have all the answers and I'm of the belief that unless it's an emergency situation, I can wait to make a decision. I may go home and sleep on it. I start to get different viewpoints and perspectives to make sure we make the right decision the first time. We don't always make the best decision and I've had to backtrack before, but that's fine. People appreciate that. As long as people know you try and correct your mistakes, they'll appreciate you.

Servant-Leaders Provide Leadership

Providing leadership means envisioning the future, taking initiative, and clarifying goals. The following narrative details Mr. Smith's beliefs and experiences with this characteristic.

During our visit, Mr. Smith shared a few of the developing initiatives for Pine School. "We're trying to start up a parent–teacher organization for next year. We've had it before under other principals, but it wasn't too successful. I've got teachers that would like to try it. They've told me, 'If we play more of a role in the organization, it may be successful.' I'm allowing them to come up with some ideas this summer about how to make this work.' Also, he shared how they experimented with additional parental involvement last year by replacing the traditional year-beginning open house with a parent orientation. "We brought parents in and had general assemblies based on grade level, then broke out into classroom sessions. Parents sat down with the teachers and went over rules and expectations. Open houses, if you're not careful, will turn into parent–teacher conferences quick. I always tell my teachers to leave their gradebooks at home. We don't want to discuss grades." Mr. Smith lightly chuckled when sharing about gradebooks and parent–teacher conferences, almost saying from experience, "I've had an unpleasant adventure with this before—I've learned my lesson."

Also, he shared how, when he became the principal at Pine School, there were constant school fights. He was proud that he clarified behavioral expectations for the students. He said, "I was not going to tolerate fights. If you can't do these types of things, it doesn't matter what happens in those classrooms." It was clear to me that Pine School had a no-nonsense, yet caring learning environment.

Mr. Smith accepts the responsibility of his position, recognizing the importance of his task. When explaining his duty to his students and the larger society, he said, "I hope our students walk across the stage and are prepared to do one of two things. I want them to either go to work or go to some sort of school. I want them to be productive citizens because they'll be taking care of me one day. I want them to be able to go out and be employable or go into college and be successful. I don't want to see them just walking the streets [without a job]."

Servant-Leaders Share Leadership

Sharing leadership means facilitating a shared vision, sharing power and releasing control, and sharing status and promoting others. The following narrative details Mr. Smith's beliefs and experiences with this characteristic.

Primarily, during our interview, Mr. Smith's fundamental perception of sharing leadership was related to symmetrical power relations between himself, his assistant principal, and his counselor. Discussing his decision-making process, Mr. Smith acknowledged at three separate times during the interview that he relies heavily on his assistant principal and counselor. Speaking of his assistant principal, Mr. Long, he appreciatively noted, "He keeps me out of hot water."

Outside of his administrative team, Mr. Smith noted few instances where he shared leadership with his faculty or staff. When asked about sharing leadership, he provided an example of shared leadership gone wrong. He said his students went on a trip and some students didn't follow expectations.

> I asked the teacher what she thought was an appropriate discipline consequence. She said the girls needed a one-day suspension. So, that's what I was going to do. I called the parents and they were sitting with their guns loaded, waiting for the call. It had already gotten back to me that the parents said their kids weren't going to be suspended. The parents came in and pitched a fit. The situation was borderline so I went back to the teacher and she was not real clear about when certain things happened. It's one of those situations where the teacher wasn't

real sure about some of the events that transpired. I knew that if I
supported this, my reputation was on the line. I needed to know
whether or not I was fighting a battle that I was going to be made a fool
of. I don't like that to happen. I don't want to fight if I'm not going to
win. I don't want to give others the satisfaction of saying "I showed
you." I called Mr. Long in. He went up and interviewed the sponsor
and got the same information that I was given. I told Mr. Long we
could support the teacher, but may not win. The parents needed to
know, whether the situation was borderline or not, that the behavior of
the girls was not an acceptable representation of our school. I told Mr.
Long that we'd go down together. I stuck with the recommendation of
the teacher. One set of parents took their child out of the school. But, I
shared leadership and asked for help. I told my assistant principal to
"help me, talk to me."

It appeared to me, that while sharing leadership wasn't considered problematic by Mr. Smith, that he did not actively engage in promoting this
characteristic.

CONCLUSIONS

Mr. Smith is a practicing servant-leader school principal. While he never
indicated he was a servant-leader, he certainly embodies each of Laub's
servant-leadership organizational model's characteristics, to varying degrees. The servant-leadership characteristics most prevalent in Mr. Smith,
based on our time together, are valuing people, building community, and
displaying authenticity. These three characteristics form the primary basis for his leadership; however, the characteristics of developing people,
providing leadership, and sharing leadership were also noticed. In everyday practice, Mr. Smith faithfully practices his espoused beliefs, especially in the areas of valuing people, building community, and displaying
authenticity. Furthermore, Mr. Smith was unmistakably passionate about
his students, his faculty, his staff, his campus, and his work as an educational leader. He beamed with pride as he toured me around his dated
school campus. From a quantitative standpoint, Pine School, under the
leadership of Mr. Smith, has made tremendous school-performance
gains.

As I left Mr. Smith's office, he indicated "This interview was fun. I
really enjoyed it." I shared my desire and hope of making a positive
impact on the educational community with this research. As I continued
to proceed toward the exit, Mr. Smith stated, "Let me know if you need
anything else. I'd be more than glad to help you." Finally, as I opened the
door to leave the administrative building at Pine School and end our time
together, Mr. Smith got the last word. He stated, "Be careful on the road,
Chief!"

ELEVEN

Mrs. Annette at Oak School

INTRODUCTION

After driving through a diverse terrain, I looked at my wristwatch. With mile upon mile of cornfields on both sides of the road and no signs of "civilization" in sight, I made the decision to call Mrs. Annette and let her know I would be a few minutes late. Unfortunately, when I began dialing her number on my cell phone, I noticed the lack of signal bars and, therefore, would be unsuccessful in my attempt to give her a courtesy call. I stared at my phone, in hopes of a viewing a signal, before remembering the old cliché "a watched pot never boils." I looked away, then a few moments later noticed one bar of service. I pulled to the side of the road so I would not lose the signal and called Mrs. Annette. She said, "Yeah, it's a little farther over here than you would think." I responded, "Yes, it looks like I'll be about fifteen minutes late." With laughter, she responded, "Well, I'll tell you. When you get to the end of the Earth, keep on driving." She, with the comforts of locational familiarity, had the luxury of joking. Pleased she was not upset at my projected late arrival, I laughed with her. She followed her *end of the Earth* quip with a sincere desire to assist me in my travel.

After arriving at Oak School, I grabbed my briefcase and hustled inside to meet with Mrs. Annette. As I advanced into the dated building, I heard music blaring from an unknown location, only surpassed in intensity by the strong odor of paint fumes. While I'm no music aficionado, I classified the tunes into an island genre and thought to myself, "How odd." As I turned a corner, I found three maintenance men harmoniously singing and dancing to the song, with paint rollers in hand. They were, much like the seven dwarfs, whistling while they worked. They were happy. I addressed one of the men, "Sir, this is looking real good. Will

131

you tell me where I can find Mrs. Annette?" With a compliment-induced grin, he said, "Aw, thanks, man. She's in there," pointing to an old wooden door. After thanking the singing maintenance man, I opened the door. The door generated a creaking sound, like many older doors do, causing Mrs. Annette to appear from a back office. With enthusiasm in her voice, she said, "I'm glad you made it. I know that was a long drive." After sharing with her, "The pleasure is mine," we proceeded to her office for the interview.

One could easily discern that Mrs. Annette was a collector of "artifacts." Her office was full of binders, baskets, files, boxes, books, photographs, pictures, and other trinkets. I was amazed at the amount of resources available in one office. She later "busted me" and said, "I've been watching you look at all my stuff." Then, she began justifying her collection. In front of her desk, instead of the normal chairs, Mrs. Annette had a couch. Refusing to get too comfortable, I asked if I could pull a chair from the side and she said, "Sure, whatever you need." Then, we began our formal interview.

MRS. ANNETTE

Mrs. Annette was an energetic lady in her early sixties. At first, I detected a strictness of demeanor in Mrs. Annette, only later to discover a softer side to this self-proclaimed "old lady." Her passionate views radiated through her disposition, and I doubted she would be overly reserved in expressing her opinions when needed. I thought, "I'd hate to get in trouble at this lady's school." Later, she confirmed my intuitiveness when speaking of student perceptions of her. "They would probably say I'm strict, but fair. I have high expectations for them. Sometimes they think I'm firm, sometimes they say I'm not. They sometimes say I'm an old lady that doesn't know anything. I think they respect me and my beliefs. I think they like me. They know what my expectations are and I'm not afraid to remind them [when those expectations are not met]." Then, she shared her thoughts on the external community's opinion of her. "They would describe me as a strong leader. I don't give in to their pressure. I look at all sides of issues before making decisions. I'm fair with the kids. I think the community would say that I'm fair and that I don't play favorites. I try hard to not play favorites and try to be fair. They know their children are safe and respected. Their children will be held to high standards. If there is a problem, we handle it in a fair manner."

Mrs. Annette lives in the area of the school. "I came to Oak to be principal because this was home to me. I was never a classroom teacher here, but when the opportunity came to be principal here, I jumped on it." She received her bachelor of science and her master of education. Additionally, she has a "plus 30," which indicates a minimum of thirty hours of graduate work beyond her master's degree. In the classroom, Mrs. Annette was a secondary math teacher for 22 years before entering into the principalship at Oak School, where she has served for ten years. "I've been doing this [education] for 32 years. I'm just as excited for school to start this upcoming year as I was the first year I started. I get excited. I always look for ways to make the next school year better. I'm looking forward to next year." Later, she added, "I think I am a strong personality. I know what needs to be done to improve schools. I can communicate with the stakeholders. I think the teachers follow my lead. I think if they didn't, we wouldn't be where we are today. They respect me."

When asked why she selected the teaching and educational leadership profession, Mrs. Annette said, "I was older when I got into education and it took me a while to get a bachelor's degree. It took me a bit. I got married, had kids, and went back. After I got my BS, I looked around and saw all these people with master's degrees and thought 'I could do that.' I knew I didn't want to get a master's in my teaching field, so I chose administration. I knew I wanted to be a principal."

Mrs. Annette was selected for this study because Oak School has achieved a high level of sustained school improvement growth. During the past three years, Oak School has grown about 20 percent in accountability measures. There are banners of academic success hung throughout the school.

Despite their high accountability rating and sustained growth, Mrs. Annette still downplayed her test scores and their relevance to a successful school. "I don't think test scores are necessarily the whole thing [in determining the quality of a school]. I can't take credit for tests scores; that's the teachers and students doing that. Test scores indicated that something is being done to get students ready to take tests. We try to give a well-balanced curriculum. We try ways of teaching that give kids success on a test, but also give them a well-rounded education. Things other than the test are important here."

DECONSTRUCTION THROUGH LAUB'S SERVANT-LEADERSHIP ORGANIZATIONAL MODEL

Following an analysis and coding of Mrs. Annette's stories, I found all six attributes of Laub's servant-leadership organizational model's characteristics evident in her belief system and practices as a principal. Some of these characteristics were more profound than others. To follow, each of Laub's six servant-leadership organizational model's characteristics will be exemplified through the beliefs and practices of Mrs. Annette. These stories, turned into narrative, form a truth and reality for Mrs. Annette.

Servant-Leaders Value People

Valuing people, in Laub's model, means trusting and believing in people, serving others' needs before his or her own, and receptive, non-judgmental listening. The following narrative details Mrs. Annette's beliefs and experiences with this characteristic.

Mrs. Annette claims to value every educational stakeholder she serves, only in different ways. In regards to her faculty and staff, she said,

> Everybody has value. Everybody can contribute. Not everybody contributes the same thing. Everybody has value and can, and does make contributions. We take each individual person and work with their strengths to make the whole better. We know that this person may be good in one area and not so good in another. We try to pull on everybody's strengths to make things the best they can be. I have forty teachers here that I can go to and say "Will you do this?" Then, they accept it and get the job done. If they come to me needing help, I try to make sure whatever they need gets done.

When talking about the value she gives the students at Oak School, Mrs. Annette voiced,

> I think if you don't have a genuine love and respect for kids, you have a problem. I found out a long time ago that if you show the students respect, you'll get it back. If they respect you, they'll do just about anything you ask them to do. I love kids by caring for them. I come across that if they want to come in this office, sit on my couch, cry, and tell me a story, I will not judge them. I'm not going to go talking about it. I respect their confidentiality. Naturally, kids are intimidated to come to the principal's office. I want them to know they can come in here and ask me things. I want the students to know that I'm a person too. I respect the students.

She also indicated her support for teachers in their quest to be effective in their classrooms. "The faculty would say I'm supportive for the most part. I'm supportive of them in the classroom. I meet their classroom needs and emotional needs. I stand behind them with their problems and support them. I support them with what they need."

Servant-Leaders Develop People

Developing people, in Laub's model, means providing opportunities for learning and growth, modeling appropriate behavior, and building up others through encouragement and affirmation. The following narrative details Mrs. Annette's beliefs and experiences with this characteristic.

When questioned about her beliefs on developing people, Mrs. Annette paused for a moment to gather her thoughts. After some time for reflection, she stated, "I strongly think you need to develop people. I encourage others and give people opportunities to further develop."

Next, I questioned Mrs. Annette about those "opportunities" and she gave the following examples.

> I encourage others and give people opportunities to further themselves. We get invited to attend a lot of professional-development workshops. The district is very supportive of teachers doing staff development. I think a lot of teachers feel encouraged to go to things and broaden their perspectives. I have one young teacher serving the state department by developing math tests and rubrics. She's been doing this for several years now. She goes several times a year. We're developing unit tests in the district for math. She's been a leader in getting that done. I sit back and give her the opportunity to develop. I make sure she's covered if she needs to be gone. She doesn't have to worry about what's going on at school. She's not penalized.

The second example involved their reading program.

> We have a reading program here. We do whole faculty study groups with that. I have two ladies who've taken over the program. They make sure it works and work with other teachers. I value them for taking the initiative to make sure the program is working. It's not easy for them. They're working with their peers and they meet resistance. Some faculty don't want to do what they're supposed to do. I value those ladies and what they do.

Servant-Leaders Build Community

Building community, in Laub's model, means building strong personal relationships, working collaboratively with others, and valuing the differences of others. The following narrative details Mrs. Annette's beliefs and experiences with this characteristic.

For Mrs. Annette, a strong school community seemed very important. She spoke of her beliefs in the importance of community, her responsibility in facilitating community, the importance of relationships, her thoughts on the benefits of a stable faculty, her feelings toward care, and how tragedy has made their school community stronger.

> This school is a "we," not a "me." This is not an "I," this is a "we." This is all of us. Any good that comes out of this school is a full team effort and is not one individual. It's very important to build community. At times, it's difficult because everybody has their own niche. I try to make sure there are opportunities for everybody to come together. There are days that go by that [those on] the far wing may never see anybody on this side. I bridge the gap and create a sense of community within this school. Everybody is on the same page. Actually, we're probably three schools in one. We have a PK through two, three through five, and six through twelve and I have to see that everybody meshes together and is on the same page when it comes to getting things done. You need to give people responsibilities. One person can't do everything. You have key people you can always go to. It helps

people to be more well-rounded and to know more about the whole program when you give them responsibility. Here, the elementary people wouldn't know what was going on in the high school if I wasn't a bridge. I'm the bridge between the lower elementary and high school.

During the interview, Mrs. Annette also spoke of the strong relationships with her personnel at Oak School by indicating, "We have a closer working relationship than a lot of schools do." She believes these solid relationships have led to a consistent faculty at Oak School. "I think that success depends on your faculty. One of the reasons we are successful here is that we have a stable faculty. Last year I didn't have to hire anybody. This year, I had to hire two because one left and one retired. When people come to work here, they stay. There is a waiting list on the elementary end of people who want to work here. As soon as something comes open here, somebody wants to transfer in. A stable faculty has been a big part of our success." She also suggested her personal benefit from her strong relationships with the employees of Oak School. "I had a lot of death in my immediate family this year. The faculty was very supportive of me and what I was going through. Everybody works together. We're more family to each other than most faculties, I guess."

With her students, Mrs. Annette frequently used the word *care* to describe her relationships with students.

> I'm very caring to the students. I just care about everybody. I care about students as part of this school, but also individually. I'm not afraid to hug a kid, dry tears, or chastise kids when they need it. It's all about students from the very little ones to the ones who graduated. I can't describe this caring feeling I have for students. I've had it for a long time. I was at Cedar High School for twenty-two years down the road. Years ago, we had a young man from Mexico. He didn't speak a word of English but came to our school. I'm the egotistical math teacher that said "math is universal." I adopted this kid, mentored him. He graduated. He stayed around for a while, then would go back to Mexico. He almost died. A lot of things happened. A couple of years ago, he called me. He said, "I need some help." He needed his name changed on his transcript. I worked with the state department and got it done. After that, I didn't hear from him in about two years. Last week, he called me and needed an apostille. I didn't know what this was. I said "Jose, what is that?" I said, "Spell it." He told me. This morning, I've been talking with the Secretary of State's office to get him this seal for his diploma so he can enter a university out of the country. He needs an apostille to go to the university in Mexico where he lives. I'm working on this because I care about him. Let me tell you another story. Do you see the sea monster–looking thing on my wall? I had a little girl working in the office. She didn't want to be here. She hated everything and everybody. She'd tell you, "I don't like anybody." I'm not the kind that allows that. I'm going to make you like me. I'd go in there and see her and I'd tell her, "I love you." She'd shrug it off, but you'd see her

smile as you walked off. This was her junior year. She had that picture in the office. I told her I loved the picture—I was being truthful. She said, "You want it, you got it." I took it and basically put it away. That was in May. The next February, on Valentine's Day, she was killed along with the student who did the guitar picture hanging next to it. I found her picture and I had it framed. I look at it every day. I'll never forget it. When I go home, all of that goes with me.

[handwritten: death is a common theme]

The student mentioned above has not been the lone student death at Oak School during Mrs. Annette's tenure.

I've been at this school ten years now. In those ten years, we've lost six students to death. That's been the hardest thing I've had to deal with as a principal. I probably grieved with them as much as they grieved themselves. That has been so hard. That's been hard. For our school, it made us stronger. It brought us together. Somebody asked me, when we lost the last young man, "Are we going to do the usual?" That's sad when we have a procedure for handling this. It's horrible that we have a "usual." What they meant was that we would cover classes for people attending the funeral. It was bad that we had a usual and everybody knew what to do. As an outcome, our student body comes together well. We don't have any bad kids here. I promise that I have no bad kids. I just have kids. They just do what kids do. The faculty got closer during those times. Everybody pulls together here.

Servant-Leaders Display Authenticity

Displaying authenticity, in Laub's model, means being open and accountable to others, having a willingness to learn from others, and maintaining integrity and trust. The following narrative details Mrs. Annette's beliefs and experiences with this characteristic.

When describing herself as authentic, Mrs. Annette stated, "If you're not real, nobody will follow you. If you don't believe, nobody will get behind and follow. Plus, the kids are not going to respect you if you're not real." Later, she spoke of recognizing her own mistakes. "I may be a successful principal because my colleagues tell me I am. But I'm still working on being better. I'm human and make mistakes like everybody else. I just hope that I'm 'big enough' to admit my mistakes."

I asked Mrs. Annette to give me an example of being real and she provided the following story.

When we started [the] reading program, the teachers needed a big buy-in. It was something totally different than what we've done before. I had to learn a lot. I had to go to meetings that I'd rather had been any place else. I had to do it. We were asking teachers to do this, so I had to. I had to show teachers that I supported them. We've been doing it for four years now and we've come a long way. I knew if our program was going to work I had to help.

Servant-Leaders Provide Leadership

Providing leadership, in Laub's model, means envisioning the future, taking initiative, and clarifying goals. The following narrative details Mrs. Annette's beliefs and experiences with this characteristic.

Speaking of leadership, Mrs. Annette voiced,

> Leadership is to have a vision and get other people to buy into that vision. Also, you must give others the opportunity to influence that vision. Leaders work to get others to work to make that happen. It's my job to provide leadership. I must be the leader. I must be the instructional leader. I must see that programs are in place and carried out. I have to see that everybody is doing their job. The ultimate responsibility of things falls on my shoulders. When good things happen, it's not because of anything I did. But if something bad happens, I assume full responsibility. When it doesn't go right, I look to me first. When it goes right, everybody does what they were supposed to do. The sign on the door says "principal." Everything comes back on my shoulders.

When I asked Mrs. Annette about examples of when she was forced to provide leadership, she spoke of improving test scores through rewarding students. She indicated that she perceived students and teachers would perform better if they knew they would be rewarded. She saw poor performance and acted, through rewards, to address the concern and improve teaching and learning. "Right now, our school performance score is good. For teacher appreciation, everybody got t-shirts. This fall, they'll get a bag of goodies. I give to the teachers and students. We reward them. We give prizes. We got a bank to donate [a] savings bond. The back of my vehicle has prizes in it right now. We gave the teachers supplies. We ask for suggestions."

Servant-Leaders Share Leadership

Sharing leadership, in Laub's model, means facilitating a shared vision, sharing power and releasing control, and sharing status and promoting others. The following narrative details Mrs. Annette's beliefs and experiences with this characteristic.

In speaking of shared leadership, Mrs. Annette primarily spoke of sharing this responsibility with her vice-principal, Mr. Adams. In our interview, she only told of sharing leadership with her vice-principal.

> I have a wonderful vice-principal. It wasn't always that way but we've worked hard to get to where we are now. It took us several years to mesh. It took us three to four years to mesh and we've been together eight years. We talk every day. Rarely do I make a decision about anything at Oak School that I don't discuss it with him first. He does the same with me. We have a shared vision and are on the same page. We get along and discuss. He handles the discipline, but on major discipline issues, we both discuss it. We've discussed, this summer,

things we want to do for next year. We have our own responsibilities, but we share leadership. We share a vision and work on that vision all the time to get it out there for teachers. A lot of times, he is in closer contact with some of the teachers because he's on duty more than I am. He talks to teachers, then comes back and we talk about it. Things like that. Our vision is to make this school better, to prepare our kids for what they'll face when they leave here. Right now, we do a good job but could do better.

CONCLUSIONS

Mrs. Annette is a practicing servant-leader school principal. Although she never indicated she was a servant-leader, she certainly embodies Laub's servant-leadership organizational model's characteristics. The servant-leadership characteristics most prevalent in Mrs. Annette, based on our time together, were valuing people, building community, and providing leadership. These three characteristics form the primary basis for her leadership. The characteristics of developing people, displaying authenticity, and sharing leadership are areas, reflected in our interview, needing additional development, based on the requirements of Laub's servant-leadership model. Additionally, Mrs. Annette was deeply passionate about her position. She indicated to me,

> I like what I do and have never wanted to do anything else with my life except be around young people. I came into this later. I dropped out of college, then came back. I could go to the house if I wanted to, [retiring from the principalship]. I'm not ready. I still have leadership to provide. When I get to the point when I'm not excited about coming to school and working with students, I need to go to the house. If I can't make a positive difference, I need to go home and leave this.

From a quantitative standpoint, Oak School, under the leadership of Mrs. Annette has made tremendous school performance gains since she has become the school's principal.

As I began collecting my belongings, Oak School's counselor walked into the office. Mrs. Annette acknowledged her by saying, "Mrs. Kristy, what's going on?" After Mrs. Kristy responded, I asked Mrs. Annette if all teachers at this school are signified by calling their first name, such as Mr. Mike, Mrs. Tina. I had never been in a school where this was common practice, with the exception of some unmarried women teachers. Confirming my belief in the strong community at Oak School, Mrs. Annette said, "Yeah, we do that here. It's always been that way. It's good because it's a little more personal." Then, very anticlimactically, I shared my appreciation with Mrs. Annette and began to walk out the door.

Epilogue

Sometimes the questions are complicated and the answers are simple. — Dr. Seuss

CORE

When principal leadership is effective, stakeholders benefit and schools become healthy organisms advancing toward a worthwhile vision. My vocational passion is molding principals into servant-leaders, capable of transforming schools into purposeful, life-shaping organizations. When we open our eyes and ears we see and hear, when we open our hearts we care, when we open our minds we solve, and when we open our arms we serve.

As evidenced through this book, effective school leadership is not only possible, but probable, through servant-leadership. This unwavering belief in a better way to lead schools is exemplified throughout the text. In a quest to seek purpose for my life, the answer is clear — serving people, places, and purposes. There are few joys greater than helping individuals or groups learn, achieve, and grow in a responsible manner. The principles of this book form my leadership core.

The decisions and actions of principals are made from the core of the leader. Those foundational values form the basis of all processing and provide shelter in the storms of leadership. When principals have a core, based upon the ideas of servant-leadership, decisions are made in the best interests of the organization's people and purpose. There is little need for self-advancement, self-edification, or self-preservation. Selfishness is replaced with selflessness, and the purpose of leadership and life is fulfilled — serving others.

Servant-leadership begins with a desire to help others by influencing their lives. In this manner, leaders add value to the lives of others. By developing the individual stakeholders within the school, the organization as a collective force matures toward the vision. The responsibility of gaining both individual growth and organizational significance rests upon the leader's core values and implementation of successful practices.

To solidify the core of leadership, the principal must embark on critically self-reflective and reflexive practices. Through this, determinations are made about strengths and weaknesses. Once these areas are iden-

continuous improvement

tified, the principal seeks to improve for the sake of stakeholders. Furthermore, the principal relentlessly quests to improve approach, knowledge, personality, and practices to become a more effective and acceptable leader for the stakeholders being served.

Stakeholders depend on principals to effectively complete their responsibilities. As I approached the end of the book, I felt it necessary to take the *principalship* back to the people. After all, the principalship is not about the principal; instead, its existence is to satisfy needs in a selfless manner. So, I'm concluding this book with a democratic practice of ensuring the voices of stakeholders are heard.

I asked a random grouping of individuals to briefly define *school principal*. Through this, their core perceptions were revealed. I provided very little clarity and requested an immediate response. The answers below are the true definitions and expectations from the people principals serve—students, teachers, parents, and superintendents. Also, I asked three principals to share their beliefs on the principalship. As you read these descriptors, remember the concept I've presented—principal as servant-leader.

STUDENTS SAID . . .

"The principal makes sure people learn and makes sure people do the right things at school."
—Preston, first grader

"The principal is somebody you can count on if you need something. The principal needs to be in classrooms seeing learning and needs to give the kids the attention they need."
—Brittany, eighth grader

"The perfect school principal is someone a student can talk to but also someone who is respected and has control of his or her students."
—Macy, tenth grader

PARENTS SAID . . .

"A school principal will always put students first with every decision. Also, the principal will listen to every concern or suggestion that a parent may have."
—Kasey, a parent

"The principal is someone that can relate to the kids and have fun with them. However, at the same time, they motivate them to excel, give and receive respect, and act as a role-model citizen, providing leadership to the school."
—Mark, a parent

"A principal must be nonjudgmental and fair, compassionate, a good listener, empathetic and sympathetic. They must also love kids, be knowledgeable of the system, work with teachers and deal with ignorant parents without losing their cool. They pretty much have to be a saint."

—Susie, a parent

TEACHERS SAID . . .

"A principal is an individual who possesses leadership qualities, builds teacher capacity, and creates a school climate resulting in quality school performance."

—Patricia, elementary-school teacher

"A good principal must accept a leadership role in the school by being fair, honest, and respected and must be a visible leader who is open-minded and consistent in decision making while defending and supporting faculty and staff."

—Louise, middle-school teacher

"The principal is the guiding force of a school with vision and discipline for both teachers and students. They almost act as the father of the entire organization, wanting the best for the family of students, teachers, and community."

—Scarlet, high-school teacher

SUPERINTENDENTS SAID . . .

"The principal is an instructional leader who is able to lead educators, students, and parents as they develop, communicate, and implement a vision for excellence. He or she manages a positive school environment that addresses the needs of the whole child. The principal is a cheerleader. A principal involves parents and community members in his or her plan for excellence."

—Dorman, a superintendent

"The principal is the instructional leader of a campus that must be able to lead students, teachers, and parents in a systemic manner to achieve and maintain exemplary student achievement."

—Jason, a superintendent

"Internally, the school principal leads the school in selecting and developing an effective instructional staff to utilize data and other resources to move the school toward its vision for student learning. Externally, the school principal is the CEO and public face of the school as a servant-leader to all invested stakeholders."

—Walter, a superintendent

PRINCIPALS SAID . . .

"A principal is a person who has a vision for the successes of the school. He or she leads the school by example in perusing professional development for self and others to reach the goals and objectives of the school. Through the process, the principal is always reaching to improve and include all stakeholders such as students, teachers, parents, and self."

—Clovis, elementary-school principal

"A school principal is a jack-of-all-trades as he or she is forced to wear many hats. Although he or she may have a favorite hat, the principal must never be reluctant to try other styles to benefit students, staff, and achievement."

—Patrick, middle-school principal

"A principal is a mom or dad to many stakeholders that need support, guidance, love, discipline, and patience. Principals perform these duties while possessing a vision to see the way and a light to lead the way."

—Mona, high-school principal

The need for principals as servant-leaders is evident in the above voices of the stakeholders. As I review each response, I see the need for principals implementing the standards of vision, instruction, organization, collaboration, ethics, and politics. However, the desired implementation method is one of servant to the people and purpose of the school.

School leadership should not be taken for granted. It is a necessary component for the schools that stakeholders deserve. While the past cannot be reclaimed, the future proposes the opportunity to lead and live in a more effective and humanistic manner. Our educational system needs quality leadership and educational stakeholders deserve principals to fulfill their purpose of serving. The principal as servant-leader must emerge. The time is now.

I've shared my beliefs regarding the principal as servant-leader throughout this book. However, my cause is only as effective as the productivity of dialogue I've created with you, the reader. In conclusion, I'm asking for your voice and a call to action for a better way of leading and living. So, now, what is your definition of an effective school principal? And, as an obligation, what leadership responsibilities do you have to serve the people and purpose of your organization?

References

The American heritage dictionary (4th ed.) J. P. Pickett (Ed.). Boston: Houghton Mifflin.

Barth, R. (1990). *Improving schools from within.* San Francisco: Jossey-Bass.

Barth, R. (2001). *Learning by heart.* San Francisco: Jossey-Bass.

Begley, P. T. (2001). In pursuit of authentic school leadership practices. *International Journal of Leadership in Education* 4(4), 353–65.

Bennis, W. (2002). Become a tomorrow leader. In L. Spears and M. Lawrence (Eds.), *Focus on leadership: Servant-leadership for the twenty-first century* (pp. 101–9). San Francisco: Jossey-Bass.

Blaydes, J. (2004). *Survival skills for the principalship: A treasure chest of time-savers, short-cuts, and strategies to help you keep a balance in your life.* Thousand Oaks, CA: Corwin Press.

Bloom, A. D. (1968). *The republic of Plato.* New York: Basic Books.

Bolman, L. G., and Deal, T. E. (2001). *Reframing organizations: Artistry, choice, and leadership* (3rd ed.). San Francisco: Jossey-Bass.

Booth, D., and Rowsell, J. (2007). *The literacy principal: Leading, supporting, and assessing reading and writing initiatives* (2nd ed.). Portland, ME: Stehnouse Publishers.

Bourgeois, N. (2010). The critical pragmatists as scholar-practitioner. *Scholar-Practitioner Quarterly* 4(3), 231–44.

Boyer, E. L. (1995). *The basic school: A community for learning.* San Francisco: Jossey-Bass.

Brimley, V., and Garfield, R. R. (2001). *Financing education in a climate of change* (8th ed.). Boston: Allyn & Bacon.

Brower, R. E., and Balch, B. V. (2005). *Transformational leadership and decision-making in schools.* Thousand Oaks, CA: Corwin Press.

Carbo, M. (1997). *What every principal should know about teaching reading: How to raise test scores and nurture a love of reading.* Syosset, NY: NRSI.

Cherryholmes, C. (1999). *Reading pragmatism.* New York: Teachers College Press.

Clarke, G. (2005). Research, reflection, and relationships: Discovering the 3 Rs of teacher-leaders. In S. Harris (Ed.), *Changing mindsets of educational leaders: Voices from doctoral students* (pp. 11–20). Lanham, MD: Rowman & Littlefield Education.

Collins, J. (2001). *Good to great.* New York: HarperCollins.

Conley, D. (1991). Lessons from laboratories in school restructuring and site-based decision making. *Oregon School Study Council Bulletin* 34(7), 1–61.

Copland, M. (2001). The myth of the superprincipal. *Phi Delta Kappan* 82(7), 528–33.

DeGraaf, D., Tilley, C., and Neal, L. (2004). Servant-leadership characteristics in organizational life. In L. Spears and M. Lawrence (Eds.), *Practicing servant-leadership: Succeeding through trust, bravery, and forgiveness* (pp. 133–65). San Francisco: Jossey-Bass.

DeSpain, B. C. (2000). *The leader is the servant: The 21st-century leadership model.* Mexico City: Grupo Editorial Iberoamerica.

Dewey, J. (1916a). *Democracy and education: An introduction to the philosophy of education.* New York: The Free Press.

Dewey, J. (1916b). Nationalizing education. Originally published in *Journal of Education* 84, 425–28. Reprinted in *John Dewey, The Middle Works*, vol. 10 (pp. 201–10). Carbondale: Southern Illinois University Press.

Doohan, L. (2007). Spiritual leadership and reflection. *International Journal of Servant-Leadership* 3(1), 281–301.

Douglas, M. E. (2003). Servant-leadership: An emerging supervisory model. *Supervision* 64(2), 6–9.

Drury, S. (2005). Teachers as servant leaders. In B. E. Winston (Ed.), *Proceedings of the servant-leadership roundtable* (pp. 1–17). Virginia Beach, VA: Regent University School of Leadership Studies. www.regenteduc/conference (accessed March 28, 2007).

Duffy, F. M. (2003). *Courage, passion, and vision: A guide to leading systemic school improvement.* Lanham, MD: Scarecrow Press.

Dufour, R., Dufour, R., Eaker, R., and Karhanek, G. (2004). *Whatever it takes: How professional learning communities respond when kids don't learn.* Bloomington, IN: National Education Service.

Dunklee, D. R. (1999). *You sound taller on the telephone: A practitioner's view of the principalship.* Thousand Oaks, CA: Corwin Press.

Eade, D. M. (1996). Motivational management: Developing leadership skills. www.adv-leadership-grp.com/articles/motivate.htm (accessed May 12, 2010).

Enomoto, E. K., and Kramer, B. H. (2007). *Leading through the quagmire: Ethical foundations, critical methods, and practical applications for school leadership.* Lanham, MD: Rowman & Littlefield.

Ferch, S. (2004). Servant-leadership, forgiveness, and social justice. In L. Spears and M. Lawrence (Eds.), *Practicing servant-leadership: Succeeding through trust, bravery, and forgiveness* (pp. 225–39). San Francisco: Jossey-Bass.

Foster, W. (1989). Toward a critical theory of educational administration in leadership and organizational culture. In T. J. Sergiovanni and J. E. Corbally (Eds.), *Leadership and organizational culture.* Urbana: University of Illinois Press.

Freire, P. (1998). *Pedagogy of freedom: Ethics, democracy, and civic courage.* Lanham, MD: Rowman & Littlefield.

Fullan, M. (2001). *The new meaning of educational change* (3rd ed.). New York: Teachers College Press.

Fullan, M. (2008). *The six secrets of change: What the best leaders do to help their organization survive and thrive.* San Francisco: Jossey-Bass.

Gardiner, J. J. (1998). Quiet presence: The holy ground of leadership. In L. Spears (Ed.), *Insights on leadership* (pp. 116–25). New York: John Wiley & Sons.

Gardner, H. (1995). *Leading minds: An anatomy of leadership.* New York: Basic Books

Goodlad, J. I., Bromley, C. M., and Goodlad, S. J. (2004). *Education for everyone: Agenda for education in a democracy.* San Francisco: Jossey-Bass.

Greenleaf, R. K. (1977, 2001). *Servant-leadership: A journey into the nature of legitimate power and greatness.* New York: Paulist.

Greenleaf, R. K. (2001). *Servant leadership: A journey into the nature of legitimate power and greatness* (25th Anniversary Ed.). Mahwah, NJ: Paulist Press.

Giuliani, R. W. (2002). *Leadership.* New York: Hyperion.

Hampton, K. (2010). Transforming school and society: Examining the theoretical foundations of scholar-practitioner leadership. *Scholar Practitioner Quarterly* 4(2), 185–93.

Hattie, J. A. (1992). Measuring the effects of schooling. *Australian Journal of Education* 36(1), 5–13.

Hatton, N., and Smith, D. (1995). Reflection in teacher education: Towards definition and implementation. *Teaching and Teacher Education* 11(1), 33–49.

Hesse, H. (1956). *The journey to the east.* New York: Picador.

Hindman, J., Seiders, A., and Grant, L. (2009). *People first: The school leader's guide to building and cultivating relationships with teachers.* Larchmont, NY: Eye of Education.

Horn, R. A. (2000, August). *Promoting change to schools and communities: The potential of the cohort model.* Paper presented at annual meeting of the National Council of Professors of Educational Administration, Ypsilanti, Michigan.

Hunter, J. C. (2004). *The world's most powerful leadership principle: How to become a servant leader.* New York: Crown Business.

Jenlink, P. M. (2001, April). *Scholar–practitioner leadership: A critical analysis of preparation and practice.* Paper presented at the 2001 Annual Meeting of the American Educational Research Association, Session 39.55, Seattle, Washington.

Jenlink, P. M. (2004). Education, social creativity, and the evolution of society. *World Futures* 60, 225–40.

Jenlink, P. M. (2005). On bricolage and the intellectual work of the scholar-practitioner. *Scholar-Practitioner Quarterly* 3(1), 3–12.

Jenlink, P. M. (2010). The importance of praxis—Preparing scholar-practitioner leaders. *Scholar-Practitioner Quarterly* 4(3), 199–206.

Johnson, J. A., Dupuis, V. L., Musial, D., Hall, G. E., and Gollnick, D. M. (1999). *Introduction to the foundations of American education (11th ed.)*. Boston: Allyn & Bacon.

Keith, S., and Girling, R. H. (1991). *Education management and participation: New directions in educational administration*. Boston: Allyn & Bacon.

Killion, J., and Todnem, G. (1991). A process for personal theory building. *Educational Leadership* 48(6), 14–16.

Kincheloe, J. L. (2001). Describing the bricolage: Conceptualizing a new rigor in qualitative research. *Qualitative Inquiry* 7(6), 679–92.

Lambert, L. (2002). A framework for shared leadership. *Educational Leadership* 59(8), 37–40.

Laub, J. (1999). *Assessing the servant organization: Development of the servant organizational leadership (SOLA) instrument*. Unpublished doctoral dissertation. Florida Atlantic University.

Leithwood, K. A., and Montgomery, D. (1986). *Improving principal effectiveness: The principal profile*. Toronto, Ontario: OISE Press.

Lowe, J. (1998). Trust: The invaluable asset. In Spears, L. C. (ed.). *Insights on leadership*. New York: John Wiley & Sons.

MacIonis, John J. *Sociology, 6th ed.* Upper Saddle River, NJ: Prentice-Hall.

Marinho, R. (2005). Servant-leadership in a changing culture: Reflections on the Brazilian context. *International Journal of Servant-Leadership* 1(1), 115–22.

Marzano, R.J. (2007). The art and science of teaching: A comprehensive framework for effective instruction. Alexandria, VA: ASCD.

Marzano, R. J., Waters, T., and McNulty, B. A. (2005). *School leadership that works*. Alexandria, VA: ASCD.

Maxcy, S. J. (2002). *Ethical school leadership*. Lanham, MD: Scarecrow.

McGee-Cooper, A., and Trammell, D. (2002). From hero-as-leader to servant-as-leader. In L. Spears and M. Lawrence (Eds.), *Focus on leadership: Servant-leadership for the twenty-first century* (pp. 141–51). San Francisco: Jossey-Bass.

Mehrabian, A. (1981). *Silent messages: Implicit communication of emotions and attitudes*. Belmont, CA: Wadsworth.

Melrose, K. (1998). Putting servant-leadership into practice. In L. Spears (Ed.), *Insights on leadership* (pp. 279–96). New York: John Wiley & Sons.

Moxley, R. S. (2002). Leadership as partnership. In L. Spears and M. Lawrence (Eds.), *Focus on leadership: Servant-leadership for the twenty-first century* (pp. 47–52). San Francisco: Jossey-Bass.

Murphy, J., and Beck, L. (1994). Reconstructing the principalship: Challenges and possibilities. In J. Murphy and K. S. Louis (Eds.), *Reshaping the principalship: Insights from transformational reform efforts*. Thousand Oaks, CA: Corwin Press.

Nakai, P. (2005). The crucial role of coaching in servant-leader development. *International Journal of Servant Leadership* 1(1), 213–28.

Noddings, N. (1992). *The challenge to care in schools: An alternative approach to education*. New York: Teachers College Press.

Phoenix Elementary School District No. 1 (2007). Job description for the 7-8 assistant principal. http://www.phxelem.k12.az.us/teach_with_us/job_descriptions/admin/ASSISTANTPrincipal78.pdf (accessed July 10, 2007).

Protheroe, N. (2005). Leadership for school improvement. *Principal* 84(4), 54–56.

Quantz, R. A., Rogers, J., and Dantley, M. (1991). Rethinking transformative leadership: Toward democratic reform in schools. *Journal of Education* 173, 96–118.

Schmoker, M. (1999). *Results: The key to continuous school improvement* (2nd ed.). Alexandria, VA: ASCD.

Schuster, J. P. (1998). Servants, egos, and shoeshines: A world of sacramental possibilities. In L. Spears (Ed.), *Insights on leadership* (pp. 271–78). New York: John Wiley & Sons.

Seattle Public Schools. (2007). Position description: School assistant principal. www.seattleschools.org/area/employment/apdesc.pdf (accessed July 10, 2007).

Sergiovanni, T. (1987). The theoretical basis for cultural leadership. In L. Shieve and M. Schoenheit (Eds.), *Leadership: Examining the elusive* (pp. 116–29). Alexandria, VA: ASCD.

Sergiovanni, T. J. (1995). *The principalship: A reflective practice perspective* (3rd ed.). Boston: Allyn & Bacon.

Smith, R. W., and Lynch, T. D. (2004). *Public budgeting in America* (5th ed.). Upper Saddle River, NJ: Pearson.

Smith, W. F. and Andrews, R. L. (1989). *Instructional leadership: How principals make a difference*. Alexandria, VA: ASCD.

Sokolow, S. L. (2002). Enlightened leadership. *School Administrator 8*(59), 32–36.

Spears, L. C. (2005). The understanding and practice of servant-leadership. *International Journal of Servant Leadership 1*(1), 29–45.

Starratt, R. J. (2001). Democratic leadership theory in late modernity: An oxymoron or ironic possibility? *International Journal of Leadership in Education 4*(4), 333–52.

Starratt, R. J. (2003). Democratic leadership theory in late modernity: An oxymoron or ironic possibility? *Phi Delta Kappan 85*.

Stockdale, M., and Warelow, P. J. (2000). Is the complexity of care a paradox? *Journal of Advanced Nursing 31*(5), 1258–64.

Stone, A. G., Russell, R. F, and Patterson, K. (2003). *Transformational versus servant leadership: A difference in leader focus*. http://www.regent.edu/acad/sis/publications/conference_proceedings/servant_leadership_roundtable/2003pdf/stone_transformation_versus.pdf (accessed March 10, 2007).

Swindoll, C. R. (2001). *Wisdom for the way: Wise words for busy people*. Nashville, TN: J. Countryman.

Taylor, T., Martin, B. N., Hutchinson, S., and Jinks, M. (2007). Examination of leadership practices of principals identified as servant leaders. *International Journal of Leadership in Education 10*(4), 401–19.

Teschke, S. (1996). *Becoming a leader of leaders, Thrusts for Educational Leadership 26*(2), 10. Academic Search Premier database (accessed February 4, 2007).

Tönnies, F. (2002). *Community and society* (C. P. Loomis, Trans.). New York: Dover Publications.

Ubben, G. C., Hughes, L. W., and Norris, C. J. (2007). *The principal: Creative leadership for excellence in schools* (6th ed.). Boston: Allyn & Bacon.

Vaszauskas, J. (2005). Successful or significant? The role of education grace. In S. Harris (Ed.), *Changing mindsets of educational leaders: Voices from doctoral students* (pp. 55–64). Lanham, MD: Rowan and Littlefield Education.

Walls, W. J. (2004). Anatomy of a collaboration: An act of servant-leadership. In L. Spears and M. Lawrence (Eds.), *Practicing servant-leadership: Succeeding through trust, bravery, and forgiveness* (pp. 113–31). San Francisco: Jossey-Bass.

Wheatley, M. J. (1999). *Leadership and the new science*. San Francisco: Berrett-Koehler Publishers.

Wheatley, M. J. (2000). Good-bye, command and control. *The Jossey-Bass reader on educational leadership* (pp. 339–47). San Francisco, CA: Jossey-Bass.

Wheatley, M. J. (2002). The work of the servant-leader. In L. Spears and M. Lawrence (Eds.), *Focus on leadership: Servant-leadership for the twenty-first century* (pp. 349–61). San Francisco: Jossey-Bass.

Whitaker, T. (2003). *What great principals do differently: Fifteen things that matter most*. Larchmont, NY: Eye on Education.

Williamson, R., and Blackburn, B. R. (2009). *The principalship from A to Z*. Larchmont, NY: Eye on Education.

Wise, A. E., Darling-Hammond, L., and Berry, B. (1987). *Effective teacher selection: From recruitment to retention*. Santa Monica, CA: Rand. http://www.rand.org/pubs/reports/2005/R3462.pdf (accessed April 12, 2008).

Wiseman, A. W. (2005). Principals under pressure. The growing crisis. Lanham, MD: Scarecrow Education.

York-Barr, J., Sommers, W. A., Ghere, G. S., and Montie, J. (2006). *Reflective practice to improve schools: An action guide for educators*. Thousand Oaks, CA: Corwin Press.

Zemelman, S., Daniels, H. and Hyde, A. (1998). *Best practice: New standards for teaching and learning in America's schools* (2nd ed.). Portsmouth, NH: Heinemann.

Ziskin, A. A., and Arad, A. (Producers), and Rairni, S. (Director). (2002). *Spiderman* [Motion Picture]. United States: Sony Pictures.

About the Author

Cade Brumley is assistant superintendent for the DeSoto Parish School District (Louisiana). He also serves as adjunct faculty for Northwestern State University and Louisiana State University–Shreveport within their graduate schools of educational leadership. Previously, Brumley served as principal of Converse School, a successful Title 1 combination school (PK–12 configuration) in Louisiana. He holds a bachelor of science in health and human performance education from Northwestern State University, a master of education in school administration from Louisiana State University–Shreveport, and a doctorate of education in leadership from Stephen F. Austin State University in Texas. Furthermore, he is the owner of Brumley Consulting, LLC, a private leadership-consulting firm servicing individual schools, school districts, and conferences. His research interests include principal leadership, servant-leadership, literacy leadership, school organization, school culture, and school improvement. He can be reached by visiting www.brumleyconsulting.com or e-mailing cadebrumley@brumleyconsulting.com.

CPSIA information can be obtained at www.ICGtesting.com
Printed in the USA
BVOW020058300312

286421BV00002B/2/P